How to Interpret Dreams

Leila Bright

How to Interpret Dreams

Leila Bright

First published in Great Britain in 1999 by Hodder & Stoughton.
An Hachette UK company.

First published in US in 1999 by The McGraw-Hill Companies, Inc.

This edition published 2013

Previously published as *Dream Interpretation*

Copyright © Leila Bright 1999, 2003, 2013

The right of Leila Bright to be identified as the Author of the Work has been
asserted by her in accordance with the Copyright, Designs and Patents
Act 1988.

Database right Hodder & Stoughton (makers)

The Teach Yourself name is a registered trademark of Hachette UK.

British Library Cataloguing in Publication Data: a catalogue record for this title
is available from the British Library.

Library of Congress Catalog Card Number: on file.

10 9 8 7 6 5 4 3 2 1

The publisher has used its best endeavours to ensure that any Website addresses
referred to in this book are correct and active at the time of going to press.
However, the publisher and the author have no responsibility for the Websites
and can make no guarantee that a site will remain live or that the content will
remain relevant, decent or appropriate.

The publisher has made every effort to mark as such all words which it believes
to be trademarks. The publisher should also like to make it clear that the
presence of a word in the book, whether marked or unmarked, in no way affects
its legal status as a trademark.

Every reasonable effort has been made by the publisher to trace the copyright
holders of material in this book. Any errors or omissions should be notified
in writing to the publisher, who will endeavour to rectify the situation for any
reprints and future editions.

Cover image © Fotalia – Andres Rodriguez

Typeset by Cenveo® Publisher Services.

Printed and bound in Great Britain by CPI Group (UK) Ltd., Croydon, CR0 4YY.

Hodder & Stoughton policy is to use papers that are natural, renewable
and recyclable products and made from wood grown in sustainable forests.
The logging and manufacturing processes are expected to conform to the
environmental regulations of the country of origin.

Hodder & Stoughton Ltd

338 Euston Road

London NW1 3BH

www.hodder.co.uk

Acknowledgements

Many thanks to all those who kindly allowed me to use their dreams. In all cases privacy has been preserved by changing names and, in some instances, gender. Personal details have been disguised.

Thanks also to Jo Osborn, Helen Green, Linda Miles, Carolyn Taylor and Catherine Coe.

The author and publisher would like to give their thanks for permission to use the images in this book.

Chapter   1: Figure 1.1 © Thinkstock

Figure 1.2 © Shutterstock

Chapter   4: Figure 4.1 © Michael Blann/Thinkstock

Chapter   6: Figure 6.1 © Mary Evans Picture Library

Chapter   9: Figure 9.1 © Mary Evans Picture Library

Chapter 10: Figure 10.1 © Shutterstock

Contents

Introduction

Before time began was the Dreamtime, when the forces of creation were active through our great spirit ancestors. The spirit ancestors were not yet segregated into human or animal; they were pure consciousness. All the languages of the natural world, the languages of trees, of rocks, of celestial bodies, of wind, fire, shadow and seed, were listened to and understood by our ancestral spirit ancestors, who used their knowledge to shape the physical universe. They also shaped our social universe by forging the laws that govern human behaviour, in accordance with their experience and modes of being.

Reconstruction of Australian Aboriginal creation story

Each of us is a citizen of two worlds. In one, the laws of space and time and the rational constraints on everyday thinking must be obeyed – objects cannot pass through other objects; the dead cannot walk hand in hand with us down the street; we cannot fly simply because we wish to, we cannot talk to elephants. In the other, we can – for a short time – go safely insane. Anything can happen. Past, present and future can converge, so we may walk not only with the dead, but also with people we suppose to be our unborn children. Our bodies can grow to the size of buildings or shrink to that of spiders. We can battle safely with lions or be beaten up by babies.

One of these worlds is the waking world; the other is the world of dreams. Each world has advantages. The waking world has advantages of:

▶ predictability

▶ solidity

▶ continuity

▶ familiarity.

The world of dreams has the advantages of freedom. It offers:

▶ *social freedom* – we can mingle with the powerful and the dead

- religious freedom – we can approach the divine and the forbidden

- freedom from the physical laws that bind our waking selves – we can fly, shrink or become invisible

- freedom from time constraints – we can become children again, or grow old in a second; we can, perhaps, gain knowledge of the past and the future.

Despite the advantages of the world of dreams, sometimes, in some moods, we confine the attribute of reality to the waking world. At other times, in other moods, we are prepared to grant the world of dreams a kind of reality too. This book assumes that the second attitude is sound – that dreams are significant and grant us a window on to a type of reality at a tangent to waking reality. In this dream reality the conscious, with all its limits, yields to the subconscious that knows few laws.

But why should it be worth trying to understand dream reality? It's because, if dreams are windows on to the subconscious – both the dreamer's unique, individual subconscious and also aspects of his or her subconscious imprinted with cultural, social and ancestral patterns – then dreams can:

- serve as guides to the inner self and thus be used as tools for enhancing self-understanding, self-esteem and self-confidence

- provide insight into all our important relationships (not just sexual relationships)

- act as informal, unpaid career advisors

- promote mental, and possibly even physical, health

- facilitate creative problem solving in all areas of life.

This book will help you to benefit from these many different powers of dreams. It will show you how to:

- recall your dreams vividly

- distinguish significant from insignificant dreams

- work with visual symbols, understanding them as a type of flashlight illuminating your subconscious

- appreciate the role played by specific types of dream – prophetic, anxiety, sexual, for example

- learn to generate dreams to help solve specific problems

- harness the power of lucid and mutual dreams.

First thoughts on symbols

Only a few pages into this book, we have already had cause to mention symbols – they will be important as we progress. So it is important to understand what a symbol is.

A symbol is something that represents something else. Sometimes the meaning of a symbol is fixed by convention or is, for some significant reason, generally accepted and understood within a society – white is a symbol of purity, the lion is a symbol of courage, the cross is a symbol of Christianity, the thunderbolt is a symbol of Zeus, etc. The visual images we see in dreams are symbols, but their meaning is rarely, if ever, fixed, although meanings may be influenced by cultural or social patterns.

Dream symbols acquire their meaning via associations within the dreamer's own subconscious mind. Unravelling those associations will reveal the underlying meaning of the symbols to and for the dreamer – that is, it will reveal the things represented. For example, suppose I dream that I am being followed home by an enormous tabby cat, with huge yellow eyes. On waking, I most clearly remember those eyes. They remind me of a time I visited Africa and saw the yellow eyes of lions reflected in the headlights of my car as I drove at night – a frightening experience, but also awe-inspiring. Cats always remind me of one of my aunts, now dead, who had a house full of them. Perhaps the dream tabby represents an older woman who is offering me something that is potentially frightening but also awe-inspiring and powerful. My subconscious mind is trying to bring this woman to the attention of my conscious mind, via the dream.

This sort of unravelling can be undertaken only by the dreamer, and the meanings revealed usually have relevance only for the dreamer. Much of this book will be about the interpretation of symbols – or determining what a particular symbol represents. For the moment it is enough to hang on to the thought that symbols are like windows, or flashlights, or two-way mirrors on to or into parts of ourselves usually hidden by other parts of ourselves.

Dream interpretation: the dreamer and other people

To say that the significance of a dream comes from the interpretation the dreamer puts on it is not to say that you cannot have help interpreting your dreams. If you become captivated by the endless fascination of dreams, it might be worth your while to join a group; this would enable you to undertake structured work in a supportive and encouraging atmosphere. If you are interested in this option, approach local complementary healing centres or look on the notice board in your local mind, body and spirit bookshop for addresses.

In clinical settings, practitioners of many of the talking therapies might feel inclined to spend a good deal of time discussing dream meaning with clients. Having said that, however, many psychiatrists are concerned mainly with evidence-based medicine and may not be overly interested in dreams, unless, for example, research shows either that a drug increases your likelihood of dreaming, or that drug withdrawal increases likelihood of dreaming – in either case, the probable explanation is that the drug, or withdrawal, interferes with normal sleep patterns.

Back to the Aboriginal

At the start of this book you read a reconstruction of an Australian Aboriginal creation story. This illustrates one culturally important interpretation of the widely recognized creative force of dreams. The passage is a reconstruction because these creation stories were not written down; rather, they were incorporated in dance and oral stories, songs, poems and paintings.

The Australian Aboriginal people believe that the experience and modes of being of the great spirit ancestors during the Dreamtime (when the physical and the social worlds were both created) resonate, to a tiny degree, in our own experience of dreaming. As we have already mentioned, during dreams space and time are unbounded. We and other beings merge and separate kaleidoscopically. In our dreams the qualities and characteristics of inner consciousness are symbolized through human, animal and inanimate forms. According to the Aboriginals, this reflects the ancestral understanding of all the natural languages and the lack of distinct categories for the human and the animal.

It is thought that the heritage of the native people of Australia stretches back anything between 40,000 and 150,000 years; by any reckoning theirs is one of the oldest cultures we know. Even at the earliest phases of human history, the power and importance of dreams were recognized. It would seem arrogant to dismiss dreams today.

Part one

Dreams: a separate reality

Dreams ... are not meaningless, they are not absurd; they do not imply that one portion of our store of ideas is asleep while another portion is beginning to wake. On the contrary, they are physical phenomena of complete validity ... they can be inserted into the chain of intelligible waking mental acts; they are constructed by highly complicated activity of the mind.

Sigmund Freud, *The Interpretation of Dreams* (1899)

A brief history of dreams

In this chapter you will learn:

▶ *about culturally diverse approaches to dream interpretation*

▶ *about ancient attitudes to dream interpretation*

▶ *about the study of dreams in the twentieth century.*

As his spirit churned, at last one plan seemed best:
He would send a murderous dream to Agamemnon.
Calling out to the vision, Zeus winged it on:
'Go, murderous Dream, to the fast Achaean ships
and once you reach Agamemnon's shelter rouse him,
order him word-for-word, exactly as I command...'

Homer, *Iliad*, Book 2, translated by Robert Fagles
(Penguin, 1992)

It is probably true to say that at all times, people of all cultures, everywhere, have been fascinated by dreams, even if such interest has been officially discouraged, for example by religious authorities. The work of anthropologists has shown that certain types of dream – the anxiety dream, the wish-fulfilment dream – are probably common to all humanity.

In contemporary, Westernized culture, interest in dreams tends to focus on the psychoanalytic, an approach we shall consider later in this chapter. Before doing so, we shall look briefly at some of the many and varied ancient Greek ideas about dreams. It is roughly true that Jerusalem, Greece and Rome were the three wellsprings of Western culture. The Bible is full of references to dreams, but we shall not consider these here because of their religious implications. All manner of seers and dream interpreters operated in ancient Rome, but it is ancient Greek thinking about dream interpretation that perhaps resonates more sympathetically with Western ways of thinking and that bears the most interesting comparisons with modern approaches.

The ancient Greeks

There are many difficulties when discussing attitudes to dreams in any culture other than one's own. Members of two distinct cultures might interpret the same type of experience, and dream, differently. Or there may be dream structures that depend on highly specific, culturally transmitted patterns of belief, which are not accessible to people who do not belong to the relevant culture. Despite these difficulties, it is still possible to learn from some of the ancient Greek descriptions of dreams that have come down to us relatively intact.

We speak of *having* a dream. The Greeks spoke of *seeing* a dream, of dreams visiting the dreamer, or standing over him or her. This way of speaking is most appropriate to a type of dream in which the dreamer is the passive recipient of some sort of objective vision. Such dreams are frequently described by the famous Greek poet Homer, who composed two lengthy poems called the *Iliad* and the *Odyssey*.

In these poems, dreams often take the form of a visit paid to a sleeping person by a single dream figure – this can be a god, a ghost or an other type of messenger. These dream figures exist independently of the dreamer. They often leave and enter the bedroom via the keyhole, and deliver their messages from the head of the bed. The dream figure often points out to the dreamer that he or she is asleep; the dreamer does not suppose him- or herself to be anywhere but in bed, and is almost completely passive, seeing a figure and hearing a voice. Sometimes the dream figure proves his or her objectivity by leaving something behind on departing. The murderous Dream sent by Zeus, the king of the Greek gods, to Agamemnon, the Greek commander in battle, fits this broad pattern. By sending Agamemnon the Dream and inciting him to battle, Zeus intended to humiliate the Greeks in revenge for a slight the hero Achilles had sustained at the hands of Agamemnon.

This type of messenger dream does not correspond well to modern reports of dream experience. But Homer also describes, or assumes, other types of dream with which we are all familiar. In the *Odyssey* he describes Penelope's dream of the eagle and the geese; this is a wish-fulfilment dream, interpreted symbolically. Penelope was the faithful wife of the hero Odysseus who had gone to war to fight for the Greeks. The war lasted ten years, and Odysseus took a further ten years to get home. During all that time, faithful Penelope waited patiently for the return of her husband, resisting the advances of suitors who flocked to seek her hand. (See Chapter 7 for a full discussion of her dream of the eagle and the geese.)

Figure 1.1 The Greek god of sleep and dreams, Hypnos, as depicted on a mosaic floor. The ancient Greeks saw dreams as visitations from deities, come to warn and advise.

Both messenger and symbolic dreams were regarded by the Greeks as significant. If there is no distinction between significant and insignificant dreams, the art of dream interpretation cannot flourish. In a Greek classification, transmitted to us by various writers, significant dreams are divided into three types:

1 **the symbolic dream**, which dresses up events in metaphors and is a sort of riddle unintelligible without interpretation. In the ancient world, practitioners of the art of interpreting such dreams could make a good living. As today, dreambooks, giving tables of correspondences for symbols, were common.

2 **the vision** – a straightforward pre-enactment of a future event. This is one type of mantic dream. *Mantic* means 'of divination' (it is from the Greek word for 'prophet'). The Greek philosopher Plato had an interesting theory about mantic dreams. In his dialogue *Timaeus* he proposed that they originate from the insight of the rational soul, but are perceived by the irrational soul as images reflected on the smooth surface of the liver. This is why they have a symbolic character. (Rational and irrational soul were technical terms in Plato.) See Chapter 8 for a discussion of modern attitudes to divination through dreams.

3 **the oracle** – a dream figure reveals, without symbolism, what will or will not happen, or what should or should not be done. The dream figure could be a god, a parent, a priest, a ghost, a living friend, etc. Oracle dreams were often regarded as sent by the gods. Sometimes god-sent dreams were thought to be seen only by favoured dreamers, for example members of the royal family. At other times, god-sent dreams were thought to be available to all. They frequently prescribed some sort of religious act that has left concrete evidence for us, for example in the form of inscriptions stating that their author made some sort of dedication in accordance with a dream, or having seen a dream.

God-sent dreams were eagerly sought and there were many techniques for promoting them – some were described in dreambooks. Techniques for promoting god-sent dreams included: sleeping in a holy place or in contact with a sacred object, fasting, self-mutilation, isolation or prayer. In Chapter 10 we shall look at some contemporary techniques for promoting desired (not necessarily god-sent) dreams.

In later Greece, sleeping in a holy place – incubation – was especially widely used to provoke:

▶ dreams containing information gleaned from the dead about the future; these were a second type of mantic dream

▶ dreams connected with health, healing and medical clairvoyance.

Medical incubation flourished as part of the cult of Asclepius. Asclepius was a magical healer who became transformed into a god. He had a temple at Epidaurus, which was as famous in ancient Greece as a place of pilgrimage for the sick, as Lourdes is today, and his symbol, or representative, was a holy snake. The sick would sleep in the precincts of the holy temple at Epidaurus and hope the god would visit them in their dreams, offering instantaneous cures or suggestions for treatment. In the morning those who had been favoured with divine visitation told the others of their experiences. Evidence about some of these dreams has come down to us in the Epidaurian Temple Record. It tells of suggested treatments, including: swallowing snake poison; smearing the eyes with the blood of a white cock; river-bathing in midwinter; running barefoot in frost; and demands for self-mutilation. Recorded cures include successful treatment of sore throats, constipation, blindness and sore toes.

A different approach to health and dreaming was taken by Greek doctors who developed a scientific, not a magical, approach to healing. One medical treatise – *On Regimen* – discusses the relationship of dreams to the physiological state of the dreamer and explores dreams that express in symbolic form illness, or potential illness. The author attributes such dreams to medical clairvoyance exercised by the soul when, during sleep, it is able to survey the body without distraction. Even the philosopher Aristotle, who was in general sceptical about dreams, accepted that they can convey foreknowledge of the dreamer's state of health. Like many moderns, he thought this was explained by the penetration to consciousness of symptoms ignored during waking hours. We will meet dreams that express, or seem to express, medical clairvoyance in Chapter 8. Many of the symbols listed in 'The dreamer's dictionary' in Part two represent the human body (see, especially, the entries on earth, river, tree, earthquake and the dead).

It is possible to give only a quick survey of Greek thinking about dreams. *The Greeks and the Irrational* by E.R. Dodds provides much fuller information and would be an excellent starting place for anyone who would like to explore this subject in greater depth. Much of the information given here comes from that book.

Having glanced at the Greeks, it is now time to turn to the moderns. As we mentioned, psychoanalytic thinking tends to predominate discussion of dream interpretation. The ideas of two men – Freud and Jung – are particularly significant.

Freud and the psychoanalytical approach

Today, if we have our own wise men, skilled in the interpretation of dreams, this is in no small measure thanks to the work of Sigmund Freud, the founder of psychoanalysis. Psychoanalysis is a combination of:

- theory about the nature of the human psyche
- therapy for mind-based problems
- a lens through which we can understand society.

Freud trained as a doctor and his scientific training was of central importance to the development of his interests and his thought. He spent most of his life in Vienna, but in 1885 he worked at a clinic in Paris where he encountered patients labelled as hysterics, whose doctors introduced him to the notion that psychological disorders might have their source in the mind, rather than the brain. After his return to Vienna he opened a practice in neuropsychology. One of his colleagues had previously used a kind of talking cure to help a woman, who came to be known as Anna O, for a variety of hysterical symptoms. The method allowed Anna to lapse into a trancelike state in which she could talk about the early onset and history of her symptoms. Many years later, Freud would take the idea of this so-called talking cure and develop it into his famous method of free association. In a clinical setting, free association encourages the patient to express any thoughts that come to mind – thoughts linked by personalized, meaningful associations that may have obscure origins. The technique aims at retrieving from the subconscious material that is normally hidden, forgotten or repressed by the conscious mind. To Freud, blockages to the process of free association – hesitating, pausing, stumbling over words, etc. – showed both the importance of the material that the patient was struggling to bring to consciousness, and the power of the psychic forces acting against their conscious recognition. Freud called such blockages resistance. Freud came to the conclusion that the most powerful forces acting towards resistance were sexual in nature, and he further linked the development of mental problems to the conflict between a sexual urge and the psychic forces acting to repress it.

Up to this point, Freud's work had focused on female patients and female sexuality. Freud realized that, to be widely applicable, psychoanalysis would have to examine the male psyche too. To this end, he decided to undergo extensive self-analysis and to make the results public. This decision was perhaps triggered by the death of his father, which released in Freud emotions that he understood had been long repressed – emotions concerning his earliest experiences and feelings. Freud made it his project to reveal their meaning by using the age-old techniques of dream interpretation. He regarded dreams as a road to the subconscious and provided an elaborate account of why we dream and the roles dreams play in our mental lives.

FREUD ON DREAM ANALYSIS
Freud published his findings in *The Interpretation of Dreams* (1899) – one of his most important books. Here he argued that dreams play a fundamental part in the management of our mental lives. He gave evidence both from his own dreams and from those of patients. Calling the mind's energy libido, and identifying it largely but not solely with the sexual drive, he suggested that this was an influential all-pervasive force, capable of extreme, disturbing power. Libido needs to be discharged to prevent harm. If denied more immediate forms of gratification, it can seek release through mental channels – a wish can be satisfied by imaginary wish-fulfilment. Freud claimed that all dreams are disguised expressions of the fulfilment of significant wishes originating in the libido – often intermingled with confusing residues of immediate daily experience.

Dreams are disguised expressions of wish-fulfilment because they are the results of compromises in the psyche between desires and forces that act to forbid those desires. Sleep can partly, but not wholly, relax the censorship the conscious mind normally exerts on forbidden desires. Because the relaxation of the censorship is only partial, in dreams forbidden desires are experienced in distorted fashion – symbols allow deeply repressed wishes to escape censorship. Therefore dreams have to be decoded to be understood.

The unmasking of the dream's disguise to reveal its hidden meaning requires the dreamer to reverse the processes through which the hidden (latent) content of a dream is transformed into the remembered (manifest) content. To lift aside the veil hiding a dream's true meaning, we must unravel, or reverse, the misleading and tangled effects of:

- ▶ **condensation** – the process by which several different latent elements are represented in the manifest dream as one; there may be no direct relationship between a manifest element and the several latent elements that gave rise to it

- ▶ **displacement (a)** – the most urgent wish is often only marginally represented in the remembered dream

- ▶ **displacement (b)** – the substitution of one thing for another, for example a witch for one's mother, a kitten for one's child

- ▶ **representation** – in dreams, (verbal) thoughts are represented in images; if dreams are to be decoded, those images must be translated back into words – one of the aims of free association

- ▶ **secondary revision** – when we recount our dream, we have a natural tendency to provide it with some narrative coherence, and may thus distort its actual, manifest, content.

The untangling processes take us back beyond the restrictions of censorship – from the conscious recounting of a dream to the subconscious wishes that gave rise to it. You will probably find you need to use many of these untangling processes in decoding your own dreams. Examples of each type of confusing effect – condensation, displacement, representation and secondary revision – are to be found in the case studies given later in this book.

Jung: the collective unconscious and the archetypes

The psychoanalytic movement has developed in many different directions since Freud first propounded his theories. One of the earliest, and most influential, critics of Freud's position was another brilliant doctor, Carl Gustav Jung. Jung did not accept Freud's insistence on the almost exclusively sexual nature of the libido and thought that Freud's interpretation of dreams and symbolism was too narrow. Jung developed two important, linked ideas – those of the collective unconscious and the archetypes.

Figure 1.2 The old man, or *senex*, is one of the key archetypes in Jungian psychology, representing, in its positive aspect, maturity and wisdom. The wise old man, or wizard, is a staple of folk tales around the world and for the dreamer may represent his or her quest to discover or question the perfected self.

▶ **The collective unconscious** – Jung held that, in addition to the aware 'I' of the conscious mind, each of us has a *personal unconscious*, consisting of our own repressed memories, thoughts and feelings, and a *collective unconscious*, shared by all humans, which causes us all to understand, interpret and respond to the world in particular, inherited ways.

▶ **The archetypes** – the deep, inherited collective unconscious finds conscious expression in universally recognized ideas, images and stories of great power. Jung called these fundamental icons of the collective unconscious archetypes, and undertook detailed investigation of how they repeatedly emerge in dreams, fantasies, fairy stories, delusions, myths and religions, all of which reflect basic human desires and experiences. Archetypal images include the hero, the child, the demon, the old man, the earth mother, etc. Jung was convinced of human bisexuality, and designated man's feminine archetype as the *anima*, and woman's masculine archetype as the *animus*. These serve not only to ensure that members of each sex show characteristics of the opposite sex, but also influence our perceptions and misperceptions regarding the opposite sex.

In practical dream interpretation, we must always be alert for messages from the collective unconscious and for possible archetypal images. Many of the case studies featured in this book rely on the notion of archetypes for their interpretation.

A note on vocabulary

We have just discussed Jung and the collective unconscious. But you will notice that in this book I prefer the term 'subconscious' to 'unconscious'. To me, unconscious suggests something dead – a block of wood, a lump of metal – or insensate – someone who has been knocked out. By way of contrast, subconscious suggests something vital and dynamic, although hidden.

Food for thought: The architecture of sleep

At the end of each chapter in Part one of this book you will find a brief section called 'Food for thought'. These sections introduce topics of related interest to the main theme of the chapter. Our first 'Food for thought' concerns sleep.

The scientists working to provide us with an understanding of the role and architecture of sleep tend not to focus on the meanings of dreams. Nevertheless, science provides a fascinating insight into our sleeping selves.

Sleep occupies between one-quarter and one-third of each of our lives, and few people can manage regularly on fewer than six hours of sleep a night. Sleep and wakefulness are regulated by centres in the brain and, although we have some control over these, sleep will sometimes overwhelm us. The purpose of sleep is not fully understood, although it is probably concerned with organizing memory. Even relatively minor deprivation causes irritability, loss of concentration and a deterioration in skills and performance. Prolonged sleep deprivation can cause depression and severe mental disturbances, including, for example, hallucinations.

On falling asleep, our consciousness declines gradually, through a half-awake phase (sometimes called hypnogogia), through loss of awareness of external stimuli, to a stage where the electrical activity of the brain is much diminished and when the muscles of the body are relaxed.

The level of lowered electrical activity is interrupted several times each night by periods of great activity when the state of the brain is similar to that during emotional arousal. These periods are characterized by increase in blood flow through the brain, changes in heart and respiration rates, erection of the penis in males, and rapid, flickering movements of the eyes. This last feature has given its name to this stage of sleep – rapid eye movement (REM) sleep. Dreaming occurs during REM sleep. During this time a mechanism virtually paralyses our muscles so that the race, embrace, fight, or whatever we are dreaming about remains just a dream and, fortunately, not an action!

The dream journal

In this chapter you will learn:

▶ *how to keep a dream journal*
▶ *how to distinguish significant from insignificant dreams*
▶ *about a woman who kept a dream diary of her own.*

The skilful interpreter of dreams is he who has the faculty of observing resemblances.

Aristotle, *On Prophesying by Dreams*

Before you can begin working with your own dreams, you have to be able to:

▶ recall your dreams

▶ recognize significant dreams – a point not lost on the Ancients, as we have already seen.

The single most effective step you can take towards achieving both these ends – recalling dreams and recognizing significant ones, as well as to making a start on interpretation – is to keep a dream diary. In essence, this is simple.

▶ Keep a pen and notebook – or, if you prefer, a tape recorder loaded with tape – by the side of your bed.

▶ Before you fall asleep, remind yourself of your intention to remember your dreams, emphasizing your motivation.

▶ On waking, immediately ask yourself 'What was I just dreaming?' This will help block interference from less relevant thoughts.

▶ If you remember nothing, ask yourself what you were just thinking, or what you are now feeling – this may trigger fragments of the dream to return to consciousness.

▶ Be patient with yourself if you have a hard time remembering your dreams – dream recall is a learned skill; you are not in a race to master it. If you never remember dreams on waking, try setting the alarm clock to go off at odd times in the night – you may find you wake at a productive time in the sleep cycle and can remember many dream images. Do negotiate with your partner, if relevant, before you instigate this plan!

▶ Once the dream has returned to you, perhaps only in fragmentary form, as quickly as you can, jot down or narrate all you remember. Do not yet attempt to decipher meaning.

▶ You may wake up more than once in the night. Record your dreams each time. Again, you may need to negotiate with your partner if this is likely to interrupt his or her sleep as well as your own.

- Later, during the day, return to your account and start sifting out insignificant dreams (see below).

- Once you have determined which of your dreams are significant, start the patient work of interpretation (see below).

Your diary

DREAM RECALL

Keeping a dream diary alone will help you remember your dreams. As you record more dreams, you should start remembering more dreams. As you remember more, you will probably find your recollections become gradually clearer and more detailed – you will be able to recall not only that you dreamed of birds, but that you dreamed of a flock of silver doves flying east to west against a thundery sky, split by orange, forked lightning.

RECOGNIZING SIGNIFICANT DREAMS

Only you can recognize which dreams are significant to you. Your diary will help you in this task by helping you recognize all the varied sources of dream content. Armed with this new perspective, you will be able to weigh in importance the content of different dreams, or different aspects of content within one single dream. For example, you will probably want to exclude some of the following:

- dreams that occur after you have overindulged in food or alcohol before retiring to bed

- dreams that occur after you have taken drugs – legitimate drugs prescribed by your doctor, or sold over the counter at the pharmacy, or illegal drugs of any type

- dreams that occur during high fever

- dreams that can be traced to stimuli, especially noises, in your immediate physical surroundings, or circumstances – for example, you dream of church bells ringing, only to wake up to the sound of the phone ringing; or you dream of falling water, only to wake up to find a tap is dripping in the washbasin in your bedroom

- dreams triggered by the current, immediately obvious state of your body – for example, you dream of the Arctic, or the desert, and wake up feeling either freezing or unpleasantly hot, or you dream of food and wake up hungry

- dreams that are obviously influenced by a book you have read, or a play, television show or film you have just seen.

Dreams falling into these categories may be especially vivid, which illustrates an important point – the immediate vividness of dream recall is not necessarily a guide to significance.

As well as dreams falling into the above categories, dreams that draw on actual happenings in your waking life in the hours before you fall asleep may sometimes be insignificant – only you can decide this. Dreams drawing on the immediately preceding events of our waking lives are common, and most of us have experienced such dreams. As with so much to do with dream interpretation, this phenomenon was recognized in antiquity. In a treatise on divination, the Roman writer Cicero noted that 'Then especially do the remnants of our waking thoughts and deeds move within the soul.'

Dreams drawing directly on immediately preceding everyday waking experience may or may not be significant. But all dreams draw on aspects of waking experience, and some types of waking experience may manifest in dreams that are almost certainly significant. These include:

- dreams incorporating consciously held memories of long-past events, including childhood events (dreams incorporating memories not normally accessible to consciousness can, of course, be both hard to interpret and highly significant)

- dreams of people we know, or have known, in waking life – including those now dead

- dreams relating to our current emotional or mental state.

Any of these types of dream could manifest in highly symbolic form. This brings us to another important point about your dream diary – it will help you to become a skilled interpreter of symbols.

THE WORK OF INTERPRETATION

Significant dreams are unlikely to speak to you in plain English, as it were. Dreams, as we have already noted in the Introduction, use the language of symbols to enable your subconscious mind to communicate with your conscious mind. Such messages from the subconscious require interpretation, just like a foreign language. The third important function of your dream diary is to help you to become familiar with the language of symbols and to learn how to translate them into a form you can readily understand. Unlike other languages, where words have common meanings, a given symbol may carry meaning only for you, or it may carry different meanings for you and for others.

When you learn a foreign language, you can make a start by learning word meanings, or by learning grammar – by learning the rules that let the language work. But how do you learn the language of symbols when there are no rules to follow – or only those imposed by your own consciousness? The answer is just to get started.

Your dream diary has helped you to recall your dreams, and helped you to recognize significant ones. To start the work of interpretation, you must now pay close attention to the images that appear in your dreams. To repeat, these images are symbols and they stand for people, things or events other than what is manifestly depicted.

Some symbolic images will be of obvious central importance to your dream; others will seem to have a supporting role. However minor a symbol at first appears, do not ignore it – all have a role to play in helping you to decode the workings of your subconscious.

To start deciphering the real meaning of the symbols that appear in your dreams – to discover what the symbols actually stand for – you might find some, or all, of the following techniques useful. See what works for you and feel free to experiment.

▶ **Set aside some quiet, distraction-free time to meditate on the symbol itself,** to see if hidden elements reveal themselves.

- **Engage in free association of ideas.** Say you dream of a hermit – what other thoughts does this suggest? My train of thought goes like this: hermit, deserts, old men with long beards, isolation, dirt, bravery, vision, foolishness, idealism, fanaticism.

- **Find out how artists have used the symbol.** Look for reproductions of great works of art, or seek out descriptions from literature. Does the artist's interpretation carry any messages for you? It might not – remember, the interpretation of dream symbols is subjective. Artists may be relying on codified systems of symbolic representation that have little to do with interpreting dream symbols, for example using a lily to represent purity or a skull to represent passing time or death.

- **Try to describe to yourself how the thing manifestly depicted by the symbol makes you feel.** Are you scared or afraid (e.g. if the symbol shows a lion)? Are you happy or ecstatic (e.g. about a new baby)? Are you jealous (e.g. of someone's fabulous jewellery)? What does your emotional reaction to the symbol tell you about the state of your psyche?

- **Try to draw the symbol** – it does not matter if you are not good at drawing. What doodles, or other drawings does your picture inspire? What does your hand want to do with the image you have produced? Does it want to deface it or embellish it? What does this tell you?

- **Look up the symbol in 'The dreamer's dictionary' that forms Part two of this book.** If the symbol itself is not covered, look up something similar, or the group from which your symbol comes (birds, fishes, etc.). But do not take the meanings given in the dictionary as unquestionable – symbols will have different meanings for different people. The symbols your subconscious chooses to use in talking to your conscious mind have meaning primarily for you. The dictionary will merely give you some ideas about what your symbols *might* mean.

- **Try to find out the role played by the symbol in folklore, fairy tale and superstition,** all arenas where elements from the collective unconscious may surface, giving you clues about possible interpretation.

When thinking about the things a symbol might stand for, it is important that the possibilities do not become so wide and all-inclusive that the interpretation becomes meaningless. For example, if you think a snake stands for things as diverse as rivalry between the sexes, sexual prowess or jealousy, healing, danger, the power of earthy elements in our psyche, spiritual transformation, cunning, misunderstanding, humankind's wanton misuse of natural resources, bitterness or poison, artistic endeavour and divine protection, you are as good as saying you do not know what a snake symbol means when it occurs in your own dream. For the most useful and powerful analysis of your dreams, try to be reasonably specific and come up with one or two possible interpretations.

Case study: India

So far in this chapter we have looked at some of the theoretical reasons for, and benefits from, keeping a dream diary. We shall now explore how keeping a diary actually worked out in practice, in the life of one woman keenly interested in her dreams.

India is in her late twenties, with a high-flying career. She is Jewish and currently single. Recently she made a major life change – moving from London to New York City. India describes herself as naturally intuitive and willing to listen to her intuition. She is able to receive messages from her dreams if she feels they relate to her psychic state, and to act on these messages in her waking life. India responded freely to a number of questions about her diary.

Question: *Why do you keep a dream diary?*

India: I am interested in how my dreams bear on waking life. Somehow they make me clearer-sighted about the decisions I take. My dreams make me view my wakeful state more lucidly. They make me surer about life decisions because they help me know myself. In waking life I occasionally get flashbacks to dreams that relate to events, people or elements that I really encounter. It isn't so much that I dream the future (although once or twice this has happened – I don't think this is uncommon), but that I recognize a house that featured in a dream, which somehow might spark off a feeling (of insecurity perhaps) that I had while sleeping and dreaming.

Question: *Can you tell me about when you dreamed the future?*

India: I once dreamed that my aunt was going to die when she hadn't been ill. She died a few months later without having been sick previously. I remember telling my mum when I had the dream: 'I dreamed that Auntie Sue owned a shoe shop and was selling shoes and had a heart attack.' My mum was amazed because my aunt really had run a shoe shop many years before, although I hadn't known this. [In a sense, this dream contained elements of divination both of the past and of the future – for divinatory dreams, see Chapter 8.]

Question: *In what form do you keep your diary? And do you record your dreams immediately on waking?*

India: I keep a written account – for me this is easier and more natural than using a tape recorder. So far as is possible I do record my dreams immediately on waking.

Question: *Do you enjoy keeping your diary?*

India: I love doing it: it is completely therapeutic and purgative. It gives me the confidence to analyse problems occurring in everyday life to which I have previously had no solutions. Somehow, my dreams allow me to take a snapshot of confused waking thoughts and enable me to identify and unravel the real nugget of the problem.

Question: *Do you share the contents of your dream diary with anyone?*

India: I share the contents only with close friends, and only if I think that I have dreamed something uncanny that relates to my wakeful state.

Question: *Does your diary genuinely help you remember your dreams?*

India: If I write down the dream immediately, my memory of it is more accurate and clear. This allows for a more accurate analysis of my psychic state. If I do not write down the dream immediately, memories of it get hazy and reappear in blurry form. I find that, if I fail to record dreams immediately and think I have forgotten them, then later on that day something usually sparks off a memory from my dream of the night before and then I will proceed to analyse its significance. [This book strongly recommends you to record your dreams immediately *on waking*.]

Question: *Do you record all your dreams, or just significant ones?*
[The advice in this book is to record them all.]

India: I record most dreams, but do not necessarily dream something worth remembering every night – I guess that matches most people's experience.

Question: *What sort of dream would you count as not worth remembering?*

India: Ones where I am in a familiar place with familiar people, and nothing much is happening – for example, a dream where I am doing the grocery shopping.

Question: *Does your diary help you recognize types of dream?*

India: Yes. My dreams often amount to wish-fulfilment exercises that really do come true, eventually. For example, when I was a million miles away from moving to New York City, I dreamed that I was living and working here, with my life under control – as is now the case. I think that was a wish-fulfilment dream come true. The dream helped me focus and clarify my real aims in life, and prompted me to start looking into the practicalities of moving, and drawing up an action plan to make the move a reality.

Question: *Do you have recurring dreams, or find that symbols recur in your dreams?*

India: I frequently dream about war, and about buildings and large structures. One of my war dreams turned out to contain genuine information about the past. I was living in Paris at the time, and kept having a dream about a battle in an historical setting, with men on horseback carrying muskets and swords. I later discovered that the house where I was living was on the site of a battle that had occurred 200 years before. [This dream contains divinatory knowledge about the past – see Chapter 8.] I also have a recurring dream about a modern-day war taking place in the stairwell of a high-rise block of apartments. There are guns, people hiding and scared for their lives, and general mayhem. People are trying to get out of the building by running for cover, but this is impossible. I myself feature in the dream as someone trying to escape – I have a suffocating feeling. This dream may relate to the fact that my sister lives in a high-rise (and I also used to), and for a while she was not speaking to me. My anxiety about our confrontational relationship is reflected tangentially in my dreams.

I also frequently dream about houses that stand alone and that I alone watch from the outside. These buildings are always white. In the dream,

I sense the white house is empty and know that I am watching for a reason, but I have no idea what the reason could be. The house is in a deserted area and, although I am not lost, I feel estranged. I think this dream relates to the fact that I was beaten up at school (possibly because I was the only Jew), and perhaps as a result I have always felt different from other people. I think I may always find myself watching houses in my dreams – perhaps because I am constantly in search of the unattainable. To me, what lies within these houses is something cloud-like and unidentifiable, and so it will always be unattainable.

Sometimes I dream about an L-shaped room that has no perspective. I am in the room, which moves and changes all the time. I get a feeling of panic that I have lost a grip on where I am and what I am doing. [This seems to be a classic anxiety dream. See Chapter 5 for anxiety dreams.]

Question: *Has keeping a diary helped you hone your skills of dream interpretation?*

India: Yes, but I think we can all do interpretations and I don't know how extra proficient I am as a result of keeping the diary. I think symbols of loneliness, insecurity, displacement and estrangement predominate in my dreams, i.e. the empty house, the L-shaped room and the war dreams. An alternative explanation for the high-rise block of flats might be in terms of phallic symbolism representing problems with menfolk – although in general I am wary of this sort of highly obvious sexual interpretation. Another theme, or symbol, that recurs in my dreams is of a rabbi chasing me in a bubble car. This, I think, represents my attempts to run away from, and my conflicting feelings about, my religion.

Question: *How does keeping a diary help in your waking life?*

India: In several ways. If I do a bad thing, whatever it might be, my dreams reflect the guilt I deny in my wakeful state. Remembering my dreams reminds me of issues and problems that have to be dealt with and forces me to confront them. I definitely believe that dream analysis helps me confront demons that I would otherwise disavow.

Question: *Did you ever, or would you ever, stop keeping your diary?*

India: I stopped keeping it once, for a few months, because my ex-boyfriend thought I was mad and persuaded me that dreams meant nothing at all. I have since moved back towards the belief that dreams are very significant and have started the diary again. It was foolish to let my ex have so much influence over me. [This illustrates that it is wise to be cautious when sharing your dreams – see the chapter on sexual dreams for more on the potential importance of privacy.]

Question: *Would you ever ignore your dreams?*

India: No, I do always pay attention to them. They fascinate me and I believe there are always messages to be had from them – except the obviously insignificant ones. For example, the other day I dreamed about the household where I used to live, in London. My housemates' dog was strung up by its front paws, and hanging from a tree. I felt terrible for the dog, but could do nothing to help – I could only observe and not take action, as if I were watching from a distance and had left the actual scene. I think this tells me I have honestly dispensed with any responsibility in relation to my former housemates, who worshipped their dog, but were not particularly kind to me. I might not take instant practical action on account of my dreams, but they do feed into my day-to-day decisions, choices and action plans – for example, as I mentioned above, my recent move to New York City.

Question: *Overall, what do your dreams mean to you?*

India: My dreams represent my peace of mind, or lack of it, always.

Food for thought: A purpose for forgetting our dreams?

This chapter has focused on the importance of dream recall. So it is only fair to mention that there is a theory that we forget our dreams for a good reason – to help our brains function by 'unlearning' unhelpful or disruptive material. The idea is that dream imagery is produced by random, not structured, stimulation of the brain. If not eradicated, the products of this random stimulation (dreams) will lessen the brain's efficiency, in part by preventing it from distinguishing between random and structured stimulation in waking life, leading to waking problems such as hallucinations and delusions. Thus, during sleep, a protective process of reverse learning works to weaken the trace in the brain of the dream. It is better for us not to try to remember our dreams, because if we do recollect them, we are working against this protective mechanism.

There are several problems with this theory. For example:

✻ Remembering dreams does not seem, in everyday experience, to lead to major loss of efficiency in the brain's function. Remembering one's dreams does not, commonly, seem to lead to problems such as hallucinations, delusions and obsessions.

✻ Many people have benefited, or at least claim to have benefited (which, in this case, perhaps amounts to the same thing), from remembering and analysing their dreams.

✻ There appears to be no direct experimental evidence for unlearning – it remains a hypothetical concept in living organisms, including humans.

✻ Life provides us with many things to be anxious about – surely we do not also need to worry that remembering our dreams might cause brain damage! This point has often been made, but it is no less valid for that.

Recurring dreams

In this chapter you will learn:

▶ *how common it is to have recurring dreams*

▶ *how to explore the significance of recurring dreams*

▶ *about studies of people who have recurring dreams.*

One night I wake up in a cold sweat from one of the drowning dreams.

Rebecca Wells, *Catfish Dreams, Part 2,*
Little Altars Everywhere (Pan, 2001)

What are recurring dreams?

To recur is to return, in thought or speech, to a given idea, or for that idea to return to one's mind, present itself again or be repeated. A recurring dream is one that presents itself to your sleeping mind again and again, perhaps in slightly different guises.

Many people have recurring dreams. A recurring dream may occur many times over much, or a lengthy part, of the dreamer's life, or may occur only a few times over a relatively short time span, perhaps at a particularly important time in the dreamer's life. Recurring dreams are almost always significant.

I have experienced recurring dreams over both a relatively short time span and over most of my adult life. Both of these dreams are linked to fears, or phobias, have obvious meanings requiring little interpretative work and can be regarded as straightforward expressions of anxiety. Anxiety dreams are discussed in Chapter 5.

As a child, I had long hair and I was afraid of spiders and insects, especially caterpillars. When I was seven or eight years old I went through a phase of regularly dreaming that my hair was crawling with these creatures, and I'd wake up terrified. It got so bad that I was afraid to go to sleep, but I outgrew my fear and the dreams stopped too.

As an adult, I am an extremely nervous flier, and I frequently dream that I witness plane crashes – sometimes over a big city, sometimes in isolated country spots. Sometimes I see a jumbo jet come down, sometimes a military fighter plane. I have never dreamed that I was actually a passenger on the crashing plane, although I have frequently been involved in the rescue operation.

My dreams illustrate the point that recurring dreams can have nightmarish qualities (see Chapter 9 for nightmares). The nightmarish drowning dreams mentioned in the quote at the beginning of this chapter can be assumed to be recurring, from the use of the phrase 'from one of ...', although the character immediately goes on to make clear that this recurring element is subject to influence from everyday current events – in this case the death of fish at a local fish farm. The character whose dream this is had a traumatic childhood. You may find that your own recurring dreams relate back to incidents or themes from your own childhood. Your dreams may be able to help you understand or come to terms with such incidents or themes.

Case study: Louise

My dreams of insects and plane crashes have a simple and obvious interpretation, but many recurring dreams are far more complex. Louise – not her real name – lives in London, works in the music industry, is in her early thirties and is unmarried. She has two types of recurring dream, linked but distinct, both featuring an identical house.

Louise's first recurring dream

Louise dreams about a big country house that she owns. The house has many bedrooms and a large garden, and it is by a river. The house is lavishly furnished and has several staircases. She lives here on her own. In the first dream her house is always full of people and there is always a party going on. People come and go, and move from room to room. Guests eat and drink plenty. At some point in the dream, a threat is introduced. Louise, the hostess, wants to get away from a stranger who is menacing her, perhaps even wanting to kill her. Often this person succeeds. In different versions of this single dream she has been shot, strangled, stabbed and pushed off buildings or cliffs.

Louise's second recurring dream

This has exactly the same setting – the big house by the river. Louise is coming home from a shopping expedition, dressed in a long fur coat, carrying various bags and packages. Some big cats are waiting for her on the lawn. They are her pets. There are lions and panthers. She says hello to these cats and then realizes that there is also a tiger present. In her dream she realizes that she does not have a tiger. This animal attacks her. She grabs it by the nose, ears or skin around its neck, and stabs it with whatever comes to hand, for example a nail file. The tiger dies. In her dream Louise feels remorse for the death of the tiger.

Interpretation

As we noted in the Introduction, the most useful interpretation of any dream is that provided by the dreamer him- or herself. This may be modified by comments and suggestions from other people, perhaps fellow members of a dream interpretation workshop, or a professional therapist or counsellor. Here is Louise's own interpretation of her dreams, supplemented by one or two comments from me.

Louise notes that in both these dream series she is rich – she lives in a big house, filled with expensive possessions (including exotic pets), and can afford to dress extravagantly (the fur coat) and throw lavish parties. In both she is conspicuously spending money, on the parties for many guests and on the shopping expedition. The house is a unifying link, both within the two dream series and between them. It is not a house she ever remembers having visited, but it is certainly one she would like to own, especially since in waking life she lives in a tiny flat. To her, the house represents security and sanctuary. She thinks the river is significant as a symbol of flux in her life – a river is never the same from one moment to the next. A river also carries things towards and away from a place or a person. In both her dreams Louise is essentially alone – alone at her party or returning alone to an empty house. She thinks this reflects the actual circumstances of her life, since she is single and does, indeed, live alone.

It would certainly seem that the parts of Louise's dreams that refer to great wealth and a splendid house are concerned with wish-fulfilment – Louise would like to have these things, or thinks she would, and the wish comes true in her dreams. As we saw in Chapter 1, Freud thought that all dreams are wish-fulfilment dreams. (For more on wish-fulfilment see Chapter 7.)

In both of Louise's dream series a menace is introduced into an apparently happy scenario. In one it is the person who wants to harm her; in the other it is the wild tiger. In both cases she has to cope with the menace alone.

The nature of the menace is different, yet in both cases Louise thinks the underlying symbolism is of aspects of her life she cannot control, hidden, powerful forces that might burst through her carefully constructed daily routine and the persona she presents to the world to throw her life off balance and into chaos.

She thinks that the underlying message of the dreams serves as a dual warning, both to be careful to remember that there are always unexpected threats to happiness, thus it can never be taken for granted, and also not to become so obsessed by potential threats that she cannot enjoy what she has, killing things within herself that might add value and pleasure to her life, as she killed the tiger. Apparent dangers can bring joy as well as trouble.

The tiger is significant because it has both a dark side, represented by its black stripes, and a glorious side, represented by its golden stripes. The beast represents both secret, black and negative forces, and positive, glowing energy. Similarly, a stranger may bring heartache, or he or she may become a firm friend, a co-worker on a great project, or a lover.

Louise thinks the party and the wild animals she keeps as pets are significant because they symbolically reinforce the main message of the dreams: to be aware of threats, but not to overreact to them. At a party a whole swirl of emotions is unleashed – there are all sorts of mixed messages, crossed lines and dual interpretations. Wild animals, even when they seem tame and placid, represent untamed forces that can either disrupt harmony or become forces for good. But we enjoy both parties, and wild animals, in their different ways.

Harnessing the power of your recurring dreams

Whether your own recurring dreams have a simple explanation, like mine, or require detailed interpretative work, like Louise's, you can harness their power to teach you more about your own psyche, and to help you come to terms with many half-acknowledged or unresolved problems or longings. If you have recurring dreams, ask yourself a few questions. Your answers might suggest ways you can use the creative energy unleashed by your dreams to enhance your waking life.

▶ **Are my recurring dreams obviously concerned with wish-fulfilment?**

If so, do I consciously acknowledge this repressed desire, and could I do anything to bring it about? Louise might never be able to afford a mansion in the country, but she could begin some financial planning that might ultimately allow her to buy a country cottage.

▶ **Do my recurring dreams link into any other emotional state, for example anxiety?**

If so, do I acknowledge that emotion, and can I uncover its source? If it is a generally negative emotion, such as anxiety, can I do anything to resolve it? If it is a positive emotion, such as joy, how can I use this to its full potential in my waking life? In my case, I could buy a book or audiotape on conquering fear of flying to try to resolve my nervousness about flight.

▶ **Do any of the symbols in my recurring dreams seem particularly forceful or resonant?**

If so, investigate this symbol in all its manifestations and see if you can learn anything from its energy. In Louise's case, the symbol of the tiger seemed particularly important. She could read about tigers, watch films about them, join a campaign to protect their environment, visit tigers in the zoo, find out how they have been represented in art, or find out about the significance of the tiger in the Chinese horoscope.

▶ **Is anything in the dream an obvious reflection of my actual circumstances?**

If so, is this circumstance one you are happy to accept, or is it one you would like to change? How could you change it? In her dreams, Louise has to face the forces menacing her alone, and in waking life she has no life partner. Louise has mixed feelings about being single; she enjoys the freedom and the sense of power that being single can bring, yet she would like companionship and the comfort of being able to share her problems and triumphs. Recognizing how you feel about your circumstances is not only a boost for self-understanding, it can act as a catalyst for change.

▶ **Do my recurring dreams stop recurring for any reason?**

If so, is there an underlying reason for that? Almost certainly, you will be able to identify a reason. Do you want recurring dreams to stop, or not? My dream that my hair was crawling with insects stopped when I stopped being afraid of insects; this was a benefit in my waking life and a benefit in my dream life, too. But some recurring dreams – for example recurring dreams of great sex – might bring pleasure and you might want to promote them rather than stop them. You could use positive affirmation as an aid either to promoting or to preventing a recurring dream. Just before you go to sleep, say 'Tonight I, [name], will dream of …' or alternatively, 'Tonight I, [name], will *not* dream of …'. For more on positive affirmation, see Chapter 10.

▶ **What is my attitude to my recurring dreams?**

Louise found her recurring dreams fascinating. I find my dream of witnessing a plane crash quite horrifying. Do you think your attitude is appropriate? If not, why not? Do you think that the mismatch hints at some underlying conflict in your psyche? If so, can you identify it? If you think your attitude is appropriate, can you tell yourself why? The point of asking these questions is to try to come to a deeper understanding of your beliefs, desires and motives – knowledge you can apply to all aspects of your waking life.

Having nightmares?

If you have recurring nightmares, and these relate back to difficulties in your past, perhaps you might consider seeking professional help from a therapist – your family doctor could provide advice.

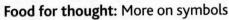

Food for thought: More on symbols

* The symbols that recur in your dream life probably also recur in your waking life, perhaps as part of the imagery of daydreams or reverie. Pay attention to your daydreams – they can carry almost as much weight as your sleeping dreams.

* A symbol is not just a symbol – it is also a thing in its own right.

* If you write, paint or take photographs, perhaps you are particularly drawn to creating works featuring the animal, place or artefact that recurs symbolically in your dreams. Perhaps your eye is drawn to newspaper reports featuring it.

* The way both the symbol and the actual thing manifest in your waking life will almost certainly link into and reinforce the message conveyed symbolically during your dream life. Learn as much as you can about the actual thing, and that will help you uncover the layers of its symbolic meaning.

Chase dreams

In this chapter you will learn:

▶ *how common it is for people to have chase dreams*

▶ *how to explore some of the commonly occurring symbols we meet in chase dreams*

▶ *about people who have had chase dreams.*

As in a dream one flees and another cannot pursue him –
the one cannot stir to escape or the other to pursue him – so
Achilles could not overtake Hector in running, nor Hector
escape him.

Homer, Iliad

What are chase dreams?

A chase is a pursuit, especially in hunting contexts, and to
chase is to pursue, to drive something towards or away from
something, or, with another meaning, it is to hurry. Chase
dreams show all these characteristics; there is pursuit and often
the pursued feels hunted or driven beyond endurance. The
dreamer is usually the one being chased – speed is essential, but
is often impossible to attain. Almost anything can be doing the
chasing – another person, an animal, a bird, motor vehicles,
helicopters, a giant snowball – and it is some menacing, but
unnameable, force.

Figure 4.1 The chase dream is one of the commonest types of dream and is
most often an expression of fear or anxiety.

In Chapter 3 we talked about recurring dreams. Chase dreams often recur – if you have one once, you are likely to have it again, or to have other, similar dreams. They are usually expressions of anxiety (see Chapter 5) or of fear, and can have nightmarish qualities (see Chapter 9). The experience of chase dreams is probably universally recognized; certainly, the ancient Greeks were familiar with this dream pattern, as the simile from Homer, given at the start of this chapter, clearly shows. Homer draws on the familiarity of the frustration felt in chase dreams to enable his audience to understand the frustration of two warrior heroes – Achilles and Hector – as they prepare for single-handed combat. The dream pattern is probably universal, but the details of the things doing the pursuing are not. An ancient Greek could not have dreamed that he was being pursued by a helicopter, or an electronic robot; a modern person is unlikely to dream of being pursued by a Greek warrior or by one of the Greek deities.

It is sometimes said that the chase, considered as a symbol in itself, may represent the dreamer's course through life, with the beginning of the chase symbolizing youth and the end old age. Some people argue that to witness a chase in a dream indicates a prosperous old age. However, as we have already noted, the most significant interpretation of any dream is that given by the dreamer him- or herself, so, if these ideas do not appeal to you, feel free to develop your own interpretations.

Case study: Edward

Edward is a highly successful businessman in his mid-thirties, married but with no children. He lives in a large city. Since early childhood he has been plagued by a recurring dream of being chased by a shark – across dry land.

Edward explains that he is phobic about sharks, and that in his dream he is always fleeing one, through a variety of landscapes, but always across dry land. The landscapes are always filled with obstacles – traffic, construction sites, tangled tree roots, etc. Sometimes other people are watching the chase, sometimes not. The shark is of the *Jaws* / great white type, with a huge gaping mouth, razor-sharp teeth, tiny, cold eyes, and a pronounced fin. It does not move with a swimming motion, but lurches along on its tail, with its enormous body vertical to the ground. Sometimes both the shark and Edward are moving in slow motion; sometimes the chase takes place at a frantic speed. Often the dream ends because Edward is frightened awake by the prospect of the shark gaining on him, or snapping him up. He has never been caught by the shark.

Edward interprets his frequently recurring dream as a warning, in a variety of different circumstances. As noted, he is afraid of sharks so he feels that for him the shark symbol represents things, people or events of ill omen. To illustrate the subjectivity of interpretation, someone who loved sharks, or worked as an environmental campaigner to save their habitats, might regard the shark as a symbol of independence, power and beauty, or of humankind's profligacy and short-sighted attitude to nature.

The exact nature of the ominous things represented by the shark depends on the current circumstances of Edward's waking life, and each time he dreams the dream, he must determine for himself from which direction threat, danger or disappointment comes.

The fact that the shark chases him across dry land and not through its natural habitat of the sea, and also the fact that it moves in such an unnatural way, Edward regards as indications that danger may not come from expected quarters. He must be on his guard and expect the unexpected. That the shark is a great white, and not, for instance, a hammerhead, he thinks is culturally determined by all the films and posters he has seen about terrifying sharks.

Edward thinks the obstacle-filled landscapes reinforce the message of warning, and the fact that each landscape is different reinforces the message that he must determine anew who it is, or what it is, that threatens him each time he dreams the shark dream. The obstacles – traffic, construction sites, etc. – represent the obstacles he must overcome to avoid the threat posed by the shark. Most of the obstacles he sees in dreams are typical of the city in which he lives, but sometimes he sees landscapes from fairy tales he heard as a child – for example, the tangled roots typical of a great, dark forest.

If there are observers in his dream, Edward believes this suggests he needs help in overcoming the problems that face him in his waking life; if in his dream he is unobserved, he will be able to work out a solution, or solutions, unaided.

Edward is not sure what to make of the speed of his dream. He has tried to relate speed to a timescale in his waking life. He theorized that, if he dreamed in slow motion the shark might represent long-term threats, or a problem that would have a lengthy resolution. If the pace was frantic, he theorized that the shark might represent an immediate problem, or an easily solved problem. But these theories did not match his experience, and he is still working towards an explanation of the speed factor.

Edward regards it as positive that the shark has never caught him – this suggests he has the inner resources to meet the varied challenges life throws at him.

Harnessing the power of your chase dreams

Just as for recurring dreams, we shall explore how to harness the power of your chase dreams through considering a series of questions. Only you can answer these questions – no one can do the hard work of dream interpretation for you.

1 What to you personally is the significance of a chase?

As we have seen, to some people the chase can symbolize the human lifespan. To others it might symbolize the glorious pursuit of worthy goals and a difficult end justly achieved – or an ill-judged pursuit of unworthy ends, which prove not to have been worth the effort. Do you think a chase, considered in itself, is meaningful, or not? How does the overarching metaphor of the chase relate to your own chase dreams? What significance does the chase have in your waking life? What sort of things do you chase in waking life? Promotion? Money? Celebrity? Or what?

➤ **Do your chase dreams link in with particular circumstances in your waking life?**

If so, what circumstances? As we saw, the setting for Edward's chase dream was often the city, and obstacles blocking his path to fulfilment in waking life were in dreams represented symbolically by the familiar obstacles of the city. Does your own dream have a realistic setting, or not? Is the thing chasing you an image drawn from your everyday waking life – perhaps a colleague or a police officer? If so, what is the significance of this? A colleague could indicate that this person is working to thwart you at work. A police officer could indicate the re-emergence of some long-repressed misdemeanour (not necessarily a legal misdemeanour) from the past.

▶ **What is the dominant emotion in your chase dream?**

Is it exhilaration – the thrill of the chase – or is it fear, even terror? Is it frustration or is it merely irritation? A chase is highly pressurized. Do you think your dream reaction to the chase might tell you something about how you react to pressurized situations in waking life – that is, to the modern bugbear of stress? Would you want to react to stress differently in waking life? If so, how would you like to react? Can you take any positive steps towards changing your reactions to stress? Perhaps you could go on an assertiveness course, or take up a relaxation therapy such as yoga or massage (see Chapter 5 for more suggestions). Or perhaps you could remove the stress trigger from your life? If this is not feasible, could you reduce your exposure to it?

▶ **Are you the chaser, or the chased?**

These two perspectives on the chase are likely to provide widely different experiences, with widely different interpretations. If you are the chaser, what are you chasing? Is it something you intensely desire, or something you merely need to catch for some practical purpose? If it is something you intensely desire, what does that thing represent in your waking life? In waking life, what steps could you take to attain it? If you are the chaser, and you enjoy the chase for its own sake, do you think that tells you something about your attitude to power or to strength? Do you like what it reveals about your attitude? If not, how could you change your approach? If you are being chased, do you enjoy, even encourage, the hunter? If so, could this be a metaphor for how you behave in casual relationships? What else could it mean?

▶ **Are you hunting / the hunted alone, or as part of a pack?**

If you are the hunter, and you hunt alone, what does that tell you about the role of solitude in your waking life? If you hunt as part of a pack, what does that tell you about the role of co-operation? If you are the sole object of another's chase or hunt, why do you think you have been singled out? If a group of you is being hunted, what binds your group together as potential victims?

▶ **What is the outcome of the chase?**

If you are the hunter, do you catch your prey, or not? If you are the prey, are you caught? What is the significance of this outcome? As we saw, Edward interpreted the fact that he was never caught as a sign that he had all the inner resources he needed to overcome threats and difficulties in his path. Do your own dreams have such an optimistic note?

Food for thought: The chase as archetype

In Chapter 1 we discussed Jung's ideas about archetypes and archetypal themes and stories. The chase is one such archetypal theme. It has been explored in all manner of contexts by people from many different historical epochs and geographical locations and has stood as an allegory for religious redemption, the glories of human love, and for intellectual and physical endeavour.

The chase, or the hunt, was a particularly powerful motif in medieval Europe, when animal hunts formed a backdrop to everyday life. One mythical medieval hunt story, modelled on a stag hunt, still fascinates humankind – it is the story of the hunt for the unicorn. The unicorn is itself a powerful symbolic image (see 'The dreamer's dictionary' in Part two for more on this). In medieval times, stories of the hunt for the unicorn were endlessly retold in a variety of formats, including paintings and, especially, tapestries.

Such tapestries, intricately detailed, brilliantly coloured and filled with symbolic allusions, were not only works of art, but served a practical function as wall hangings in draughty buildings. Unicorn tapestries might show a group of noblemen setting out on the hunt, accompanied by their hunting dogs, and then the unicorn at bay, perhaps in a stream, being attacked from all sides by huntsmen and dogs. Next, the unicorn might be shown attempting to defend itself, using both its hooves and its horn. The hunters may be deterred by the ferocity of the unicorn's defence, and resort to a ruse to capture it – the ruse of a virgin maiden, popularly believed to be able to capture a unicorn. Such a scene was often depicted. Tapestries might show the end of the hunt in various ways, either with the unicorn being captured and killed, or being kept in relatively peaceful captivity.

Stories of the hunt for the unicorn were at one and the same time allegories of both Christian love (the unicorn representing Christ) and human love, in which the unicorn represented a lover–bridegroom. The redeeming power of love (religious or human) is a theme that speaks as loudly to us today as it did when unicorn tapestries were brand new. Your chase dreams might form contemporary allegories for either or both of these themes.

Anxiety dreams

In this chapter you will learn:

▶ *to harness the power of anxiety dreams*
▶ *about the different types of anxiety dream*
▶ *stress-busting techniques.*

Worrying is the most natural and spontaneous of all human functions. It is time to acknowledge this, perhaps even to learn to do it better.

Lewis Thomas, *More Notes of a Biology Watcher* (1979)

What are anxiety dreams?

Unfortunately, most of us recognize anxiety; it is a common hazard of modern life, and up to 25 per cent of patients seen by family doctors complain of problems stemming from anxiety. Symptoms can range from insomnia to irritable bowel syndrome, or from excess sweating to breathing problems.

Anxiety is a natural response to real or perceived danger. Unhappily, it often occurs in the absence of an obvious cause – with destructive consequences. There is much debate about the roots of anxiety. Freud thought it originated with the baby's perception of the trauma of being born. Others suggest that it may be due to the overstimulation of the infant's mind, to which experiences come faster than they can be organized and understood. The conflict between external demands and internal drives may explain anxiety, or it may be a result of early, systematic attempts to avoid events or things perceived as causes of pain.

Perhaps most optimistically, from the dream interpreter's point of view, some cognitive psychologists believe that anxiety results from the way a person interprets a situation. They believe that a full explanation and reappraisal can dispel anxiety – a process that can surely be aided by unmasking how and why anxiety manifests in our dreams. Let's put it this way: if it is really time to learn to do our worrying better, as the quotation given above would have it, then harnessing the power of anxiety dreams is one possible place to start!

Many anxiety dreams have obvious causes in our waking lives and require little in-depth analysis. When I was working full time in an office, anxiety at work was frequently reflected in my dreams – most commonly in a scenario where I was frantically, yet hopelessly, searching for one vital piece of paper on a desk overflowing with bits of paper, in an office strewn with yet more papers.

Work is an ongoing stress trigger, and this dream, like many anxiety dreams, was recurring (see Chapter 3). But sometimes specific, short-term, stressful situations or events in our waking lives can be reflected in anxiety dreams. As an example, one correspondent reported that in the run-up to her wedding she dreamed that the day arrived and she had still not bought a dress or any accessories. This clearly reflected the organizational pressures she felt at the time.

In another example Jane, a high-flying career woman in her late twenties, reported that when she was buying a house – a slow and painful process – she dreamed one night that the roof of the property she was trying to buy fell off, leaving only bare planks of wood. Interestingly, her father interpreted this dream as a warning and advised her against buying that particular house, but Jane herself, rather than interpreting the dream as predictive, thought it merely reflected her obvious anxiety, and went ahead with the purchase. She is now happy in her house, which shows once again that the most important interpretation of a dream is that put on it by the dreamer him- or herself, and not the possible interpretations suggested by other people.

Marrying and moving are both major life changes, as is becoming a parent for the first time. This, though wonderful, brings a whole host of new worries. One new father reported that soon after his daughter was born he dreamed she looked like a baby, but began spouting foul language like an adult. He put this down to his anxiety that he might fail her as a father, resulting in her becoming an unhappy, poorly socialized adult who would be disappointed with her life.

Some anxiety dreams require far more interpretative work than any of the examples given above. The following case studies illustrate two more complex dreams, one manifesting personal anxiety about a family situation, the other political anxiety about the fate of humans and the planet.

Case studies: Mary and Louise
Personal anxiety dream

Mary is married with two preschool children. She is in her mid-thirties and does not take paid employment outside the home.

Mary often dreams about her children. One night she dreamed that her family had gone on an unlikely sort of skiing holiday. Mary has been skiing only twice, and is not a good skier. The family was staying in a building that seemed familiar, although Mary could not quite place it – it was most like a prefabricated classroom, or a building of that sort – certainly not a skiing chalet. Around the building were planted a mass of bushes, such as are typical of municipal parks. The ground was on a slight slope – not a mountain – and just outside their door a few steps led down a path. The ground was covered in snow and ice.

In the dream Mary's little boy, who was not wearing winter clothing, fell down the steps and began sliding away from Mary, down the slight hill, which got steeper and steeper as Mary watched. Mary tried to follow after her son, but could not – something restrained her. Her son did not appear to be coming to any physical harm through his fall, and did not cry out, but nevertheless Mary woke up with a shock, terribly afraid for her son.

The child can be an archetypal figure, representing a carefree innocence and an unfettered curiosity to which we all respond. But in this case the child was Mary's own little boy – a particular person with a particular relationship to her. All mothers worry about their children's development and future, about their own performance as mothers, and about how their family is functioning as a whole. Mary interpreted her dream as an expression of these maternal anxieties.

She thought the fact that the dream was set in a most unlikely skiing setting was a symbolic way of recognizing that she cannot anticipate all that the world will throw at her son. He will live in an environment that is in many ways alien to her, or at least separate from her, for much of his life – school, work, his own family, etc.

Mary thought that her son falling away from her was a symbolic representation of the fact that every minute they are alive children are hurtling away from their mothers – away from their mother's body, away from their mother as a possible source of food, and away from the security of their home to a dangerous, but necessary and exciting, independence. Mary thought that, because she was powerless to follow her son, this was a manifestation of the fact that she must come to recognize, accept and even welcome her son's independence, and not try to impede it.

Because her son did not appear to be coming to any harm through his fall and did not cry out, Mary took these as comforting signs, or good omens. Her son was relishing his growing independence and freedom. He felt no need to call to her to rescue him. It did not seem to matter that he was inappropriately dressed for the snow – this was a sign, she thought, that he was often more robust than she gave him credit for.

The prefabricated, classroom-like buildings and the municipal planting typical of a park Mary interpreted as the memories of her own childhood that she brought to her own experience as a parent. Sometimes her childhood memories were only half acknowledged – she could not quite place the buildings – but they were always powerful and influenced her behaviour as a mother.

Mary felt that her dream, although an expression of deep and natural parental anxiety, also offered her a key to understanding and coming to terms with the implications of that anxiety, once she had fully interpreted it.

Political anxiety dream

Dreams of war and mass destruction, which may be interpreted as expressing a generalized political anxiety, as opposed to a personal anxiety, are common. One person I spoke to had a dream in which the Earth was about to be destroyed by a huge asteroid in the shape of a house. He watched, helpless to defend himself, as politicians announced impending doom over the television. (This dream predated a spate of high-profile asteroid-impact movies, and was thus not influenced by them.)

Louise, whom we first met in Chapter 3, had a detailed dream of mass destruction. She was driving into London with one of her favourite aunts. There were crowds of people filling the roads, making driving impossible. Eventually Louise and her aunt abandoned the car. Louise recognized many of the people in the crowds as childhood friends, now grown up. Louise and her aunt tried to enter the Underground. As they went down, they passed several archways filled with big black birds – crows or ravens. Portcullises dropped in front of the birds, which started fighting. Louise and her aunt couldn't get into the Underground because it was full of people, so they returned to street level, where it was now getting dark. It was very hot, with hot winds blowing. There were trains travelling through the sky, supported by some sort of huge network, not of rails but of lights or lasers. There was an enormous explosion above the network and debris started to fall through it, making it spark and flash and throwing an eerie light. Far away in the distance, but still within the network, Louise saw a huge fireball coming towards her – then she was woken by her roommate.

Louise, who is politically aware and a member of several campaigning and environmental organizations, interpreted this dream as one of anxiety concerning impending mass destruction or disaster on a vast scale. She felt cheated that her roommate woke her before the dream's end, as she would like to have known how the dream progressed.

Like the child, the aunt can be an archetypal figure, a manifestation of the wise woman – at once virgin, mother and crone, part healer, part mystic, part goddess. Louise felt that it was highly significant that it should be her aunt, considered in these abstract terms, who accompanied her through this dream. She also thought it significant that she saw images of her childhood friends, now grown up – people she had known and loved were in danger.

Tunnels (and, for that matter, trains and explosions) are frequently thought to carry a sexual symbolism, but Louise thought this was highly unlikely in this case. Rather, she felt that the Underground represented safety and shelter. She and her aunt could not get in, signifying the overwhelming and unavoidable nature of the danger. In waking life, Louise is scared of birds and thought they were an unlucky portent in her dream.

Heat is associated with explosions of all kinds, and hot winds with nuclear explosions in particular. The trains and lasers Louise took to represent human technology. The fact that these were in the sky she took to represent both the inappropriate use of human technology and humankind's reckless attempt to subdue all aspects of the natural world. The fireball represented humanity's power to destroy itself.

Louise understood her dream as both an expression of her anxieties about our ability to destroy ourselves, and a call to action to try to do what she could to persuade others to adopt her pacifist views and her care for the environment.

Harnessing the power of your anxiety dreams

As we have seen, dream interpretation can offer a powerful shortcut to recognizing deep-seated fears and anxieties. The most helpful step you can take is to unmask the symbols in your dream in a systematic way, following the examples of Mary and Louise. Then try to answer the following questions, to help combat your anxiety.

▶ **Does my dream suggest a practical course of action that would either help reduce my anxiety, or at least help me to live with it?**

Louise's dream suggested that she should continue her political activities.

▶ **Does my dream highlight positive aspects of my anxiety?**

Mary's dream showed the dual nature of maternal anxiety, necessary as part of the love a mother feels for her child, but something that must be overcome if that child is to reach a fulfilling independence. Mary's dream helped her to recognize that she must in some sense let go – a recognition that worked for positive benefit in her psyche.

▶ **Does my dream suggest any people who might help me to resolve my anxieties?**

Possibly your dream will feature either an archetypal figure, perhaps an old man or an old woman, hinting at someone you could approach for help in waking life, or someone actually known to you in waking life.

▶ **Does my dream suggest an ill-founded anxiety that I could eradicate entirely?**

Sometimes, working with dreams will help you recognize that your worry is unfounded, and thus you will be able to eliminate it. For example, suppose you are worried about your financial situation and this is reflected in your dreams, perhaps in images of great poverty, or even in images of wealth and profligacy. Once fully understood, such dreams might prompt you to undertake a full review of your finances, which might plausibly reveal that you are worrying unnecessarily.

▶ **If the cause of my anxiety dreams is immediately obvious, could I change my waking life to eradicate that cause?**

Perhaps work-related anxiety dreams could prompt you to review your working practices. Perhaps you could work at home some of the time, delegate a few responsibilities, or even make radical changes such as swapping to part-time working.

▶ **What do my anxiety dreams say about my personality as a whole?**

Some people seem to thrive on worry – it seems they are not happy unless they are worried; others are literally made ill by worry. Some people love risk; others hate it. Some people enjoy drama and crisis in their lives; others like a quiet life. What sort of person are you? Are you happy with your anxiety personality profile? If not, how could you change it?

Food for thought: Stress-busting, anxiety reduction plan

If stress or anxiety is making you miserable, many complementary therapies can help. Here is a brief résumé. For more detailed advice, consult the complementary practitioners of your choice. Whatever their speciality, they will be able to offer you guidance and support.

* **Massage** has psychological as well as physical benefits and can reduce stress and anxiety. Many types of massage are available, for example Swedish, shiatsu and aromatherapy massage.

* **Aromatherapy** – the art of using aromatic essential oils extracted from plants for healing purposes – can work on the mind as well as the body. Lavender oil is one of the safest and easiest to use and is widely available in health stores. Put a few drops in your bath before you go to bed to help ensure a good night's sleep.

* **Bach Flower Remedies** are another possibility – these are made by steeping parts of plants in water and alcohol, leaving an energy imprint in the solution. Bach Flower Remedies are particularly useful in balancing emotional and psychological upsets.

* Many **homoeopathic remedies** are available to help you overcome stress, anxiety and depression. Their precise use depends upon the specific details of your case. Homoeopathy works on the principle that a substance that produces symptoms similar to those you show will help to cure your problem.

* **Yoga** and **t'ai chi** both help bring peace to an unquiet mind. Both combine movement and breathing exercises.

* **Reflexology** is a type of foot massage that relies on the theory that zones of the body are reflected on the feet. Reflexologists are often skilled in helping you to combat psychological upset.

* Finally, do not overlook the importance of **breathing.** In the West, we tend to ignore the process of breathing, but it is fundamental not only to life but also to mental happiness. Try to become conscious of your breathing. Breathe slowly and deeply, filling both lungs, then expelling all the air. This is generally safe, but if you experience any ill effects, such as giddiness or light-headedness, stop at once.

Sexual dreams

In this chapter you will learn:

▶ *about dreams and wish-fulfilment*
▶ *to consider the relationship between sexual dreams and sexual fantasy*
▶ *to consider the pros and cons of sharing sexual dreams and sexual fantasies.*

Sweet dreams are made of this.

Eurhythmics, song lyric (1983)

What are sexual dreams?

Whether you think that sex is the sole joy in life or less satisfying than a cup of tea, the root of our entire psychological make-up or nothing but a biological mechanism for mixing up genes, whether you think it is dirty, dangerous and deplorable, or dirty, wonderful and fun, it is difficult to ignore it – in either the waking or the dream worlds.

Most of us probably do dream about sex at some time, but analysing sexual dreams can present the dreamer with special difficulties. These can be because he or she is afraid to confront issues that may be inherent in, or revealed by, his or her dreams, or because he or she feels guilt associated with his or her dreams. Alternatively, there may be some other deep-seated reason connected with psychic protection – perhaps the dreamer regards the dream as degrading or pornographic.

For example, one person I talked to while researching this book said she often dreamed of being raped by a robot at the side of a road. This dream would seem pregnant with meaning, but the dreamer was not willing to analyse it deeply. A man I spoke to, who is happily married, said he often had explicit, erotic sexual dreams in which he was the dominant, aggressive partner, but on waking he was never entirely sure that his partner had been his wife – he did not know who it was. He feels guilty about these dreams – he thinks he is being disloyal in his sleep – and is thus unwilling to explore them further.

Despite these difficulties, plus the additional complication that there is perhaps no symbol incapable of representing sexual acts or wishes, it would seem worth while to try to understand our sexual dreams. Therapists and relationship counsellors agree that one of the keys to a healthy and happy sexual relationship is good communication between the partners. An important component of communication is listening – if we never listen to our partners, we can never hope to understand them.

Dream interpretation can be regarded as communication with oneself, so by analogy we need to listen to what our dreams are saying to us if we are to understand ourselves.

Among other things, understanding ourselves means revealing aspects of our personalities usually censored by social convention, as well as revealing hidden needs, wants and desires. Self-understanding is a key plank in building and maintaining a happy sexual relationship, or to ensuring mental wellbeing if we choose to remain single.

Case study: Otto Rank

Given the difficulties of collecting dreams with a sexual content, we shall here discuss one of the dreams recounted by Freud in his classic work *The Interpretation of Dreams* – a book well worth continued study. The dream was originally reported and interpreted by Freud's colleague Otto Rank in 1911.

The dream

A man dreamed he was running down a staircase of an apartment block, chasing a little girl who had done something to him and whom he wanted to punish. He flew down the stairs, his feet not touching the treads. At the foot of the stairs someone stopped the little girl for him. He caught hold of the child and found himself engaged in sexual activity with her, in the middle of the stairs but, as it were, in the air. It was not penetrative sex; rather the grown man was rubbing his genitals against the little girl's external genitalia, which he could see extremely distinctly, along with the girl's head. During the sexual act he saw hanging above him two small landscapes, representing a house surrounded by trees. At the bottom of the smaller picture he saw, not the artist's signature, but his own name, as if the picture were intended as a birthday gift for him. A label in front of the two pictures explained that cheaper ones were also available. He then saw himself indistinctly, as if he were lying in bed on the landing, and was woken up by the sensation of wetness caused by an ejaculation.

Interpretation

In this dream Rank saw several connections with actual events of the previous day, which appeared in the dream content. (Remember to be alive to such connections when interpreting your own dreams.) On the day of the dream the dreamer had been in a bookshop, and some landscapes, similar to those in the dream, had caught his eye. Thus Rank thought the presence of the pictures was largely explained. (He thought the pictures carried some additional meanings, linking in to Freud's wider theories, but these links need not concern us here.) Later in the evening, the dreamer had heard a story about a servant girl who had said that her illegitimate child had been 'made on the stairs' (i.e. conceived on the stairs). Rank thought this experience also fed into the dream.

Rank also thought the dream incorporated fragments of infantile recollection. The staircase was from the house where the dreamer had spent the greater part of his childhood, and where he had first 'made conscious acquaintance with the problems of sex'. As a boy, he had frequently played on these stairs and sliding down the banisters had aroused him sexually. In the dream, too, he rushed down the stairs very fast. Thus Rank suggested that the beginning of the dream represented sexual excitement. The dreamer had also often played with neighbourhood children on the stairs and had satisfied his desires in just the way he did in the dream.

Before progressing further, we need to know that Freud thought that 'Steps, ladders or staircases, or as the case may be, walking up or down them, are representations of the sexual act' and explained 'It is not hard to discover the basis of the comparison: we come to the top in a series of rhythmical movements and with increasing breathlessness and then, with a few rapid leaps, we can get to the bottom again. Thus the rhythmical pattern of copulation is reproduced...'

Rank drew on Freud's understanding of the meaning of staircases to conclude that the meaning of the dream was quite transparent, its motivating force being revealed by the ejaculation that was its outcome, and suggested that this dream provided evidence that Freud was right in his interpretation of staircases. (It might strike you that Rank seems relatively uninterested in the potentially sadistic elements in this dream.) Rank reported:

> The dreamer's sexual excitement was awakened during his sleep – this being represented in the dream by his rushing down the stairs. The sadistic element in the sexual excitement, based on the romping in his childhood, was indicated by the pursuit and overpowering of the child. The libidinal excitement increased and pressed towards sexual

action – represented in the dream by his catching hold of the child and conveying it to the middle of the stairs... But symbolic satisfaction of that kind was not enough... The excitation led to an orgasm and thus revealed the fact that the whole staircase symbolism represented copulation... [This dream offers confirmation of] Freud's view that one of the reasons for the use of going upstairs as a sexual symbol is the rhythmical character of both activities: for the dreamer expressly stated that the most clearly defined element in the whole dream was the rhythm of the sexual act, and its up-and-down motion.

A dream that ends in ejaculation is fairly obviously sexual in nature – although Rank also linked it to the infantile experience of bedwetting. Freud also reports a number of dreams where the sexual content is far more ambiguous. For example, one of his patients reported a dream in which she was wearing a peculiarly shaped hat whose 'middle piece was bent upwards, and its side pieces hung downwards'. Freud interprets this as symbolic of the male genitalia, and linked the dream to his patient's agoraphobia.

As we have already mentioned, almost any symbol can stand for sexual needs, facts or wishes. It is important to remember this when interpreting your own dreams, and to uncover the possibly unique meanings that symbols have for you. Remember that the most significant interpretation that can be placed on your dreams is that which you produce yourself. If you dream of a staircase, or whatever, and know that Freud thought it represented sex, do not feel bound to place a sexual interpretation on your dream. (See Louise's political anxiety dream in Chapter 5 for a non-sexual interpretation of symbols traditionally thought to represent sex.)

Harnessing the power of your sexual dreams

When working with the energy and creative force of sexual dreams, ask yourself the following questions:

➤ **Why do particular symbols carry a sexual connotation for me?**

What is the significance of this? Do my own sexual symbols have their prototypes in my childhood, or in more recent experience?

Figure 6.1 In traditional European belief, sexual dreams were considered as visits from terrifying demons – female succubi and male incubi. Repeated visits from such demons were thought to lead to illness or even death.

▶ **What is the dominant emotion in my sexual dreams, and why and how does this relate to my sex life?**

▶ **Do I feel guilty about my sexual dreams?**

If so, why?

▶ **Can I discuss my dreams with my partner (if relevant)?**

If not, why not?

▶ **Would any benefits accrue from sharing my dreams with him/her?**

If so, what would they be? A practical, or technical, enhancement of our sex life? Or a deeper level of emotional commitment to each other? Or what?

▶ **Do I have strong reasons for keeping my dreams private?**

For example, do I think their content might upset or disturb my partner? Do I want to reveal my dreams, or not? Is their privacy essential to me? Would revealing my dreams upset the balance of my relationship? Remember that part of skilful communication is knowing when to keep silent.

▶ **Would I engage in acts depicted in my dreams in waking life?**

If not, why not? Some acts, of course, remain exciting only so long as they are not acted out in reality. Many such acts might be depicted in our dreams, where no social or other constraints apply.

▶ **Are any acts in my dreams examples of wish-fulfilment?**

If so, could I fulfil them in waking life, without degrading, humiliating or exploiting another person? What is stopping me? (If your dreams are examples of sadistic, violent or exploitative wish-fulfilment, they will have to remain in the realm of wishes. If you are worried by such dreams, seek professional advice.)

▶ **Do I enjoy my sexual dreams, or not?**

Do they in any sense meet needs not met in my waking sex life? Would it help to talk my needs over with my partner (if relevant)? If not, does the block to communication serve a useful protective purpose, or is it destructive? If destructive, how could we overcome the blockage?

The purpose of these questions, and of attempting the difficult task of providing yourself with an honest and forthright interpretation of your sexual dreams, is to open up a dialogue with yourself in a highly charged area fraught with danger and difficulty. There are no right or wrong answers, but our dreams can help us understand parts of ourselves usually hidden from both the world and our waking selves. They can bring to consciousness hidden motives and needs that, once revealed, can – if we so desire and deem appropriate – feed into our waking sex lives to our own benefit, and to the benefit of our partners and our relationships.

Seek advice

If your dreams reflect persistent, deep-seated sexual problems or relationship difficulties, seek the advice of a professional therapist or counsellor. Your family doctor is a good source of information and advice.

Food for thought: Sexual fantasy

Dreams and fantasies both derive from parts of ourselves not subject to the normal codes and conventions of behaviour – both are free of social censorship. Our waking sexual fantasies can be as useful as dreams as tools for revealing our hidden sexual natures. Like dreams, fantasies reveal aspects of our personalities not usually on public view.

Whatever their content, you need to think as carefully about revealing your sexual fantasies to your partner as you do about revealing your sexual dreams. Like some dreams, some fantasies are exciting only when not put into practice. If your fantasies feature sex with someone other than your regular partner, it might not be tactful to mention this. If they feature sadomasochistic bondage, for example, you might feel that your partner would be disturbed by this. Before taking the plunge and telling your partner you'd like him/her to dress up as a schoolboy/girl and give you the cane, think about why you might reveal your sexual fantasies – do you see this as a first step to acting them out, or not? Would your partner be happy to act them out, do you think? Do you want your partner to tell you his or her fantasies? Do you think he or she would want to do this, or not?

This is not to say you should not share your sexual fantasies, or, for that matter, your dreams. Sharing them can bring you closer to your partner – you are likely to discover aspects of each other's personalities that you have previously kept hidden from each other. What you discover about each other's sexual tastes and preferences can be used to enhance your regular lovemaking. Talking about fantasies could be a first step to developing a bond of trust that would free you to explore a much more adventurous sex life, incorporating fantasy elements. At the very least, talking about fantasies can be arousing, and a useful way of enhancing foreplay.

If your partner asks you to engage in acts that you feel unhappy about, for any reason, never feel afraid to say no. Never engage in sexual bullying. Beware of pushing either dreams or fantasies too far.

Wish-fulfilment dreams

In this chapter you will learn:

▶ *more about wish fulfilment*
▶ *about one of the most famous dreams of any dreamer, ever*
▶ *about wish-fulfilment and waking dreams.*

Little Bo-peep has lost her sheep,
And doesn't know where to find them.
Leave them alone, and they'll come home,
Bringing their tails behind them.
Little Bo-peep fell fast asleep,
And dreamed she heard them bleating.
But when she awoke, she found it a joke,
For they were still afleeting.

Nursery rhyme

What are wish-fulfilment dreams?

As we mentioned in Chapter 1, Freud thought all dreams concerned wish fulfilment. He wrote: 'When the work of interpretation has been completed, we perceive that a dream is a fulfilment of a wish.'

We don't necessarily have to accept that all dreams concern wish fulfilment to agree that many of them do. Little Bo-peep lost her sheep, fell asleep and dreamed she heard them bleating – a clear example of wish fulfilment! Interestingly, this children's rhyme assumes familiarity with the wish-fulfilment dream pattern in even the youngest children – otherwise they would not be able to understand the significance of Bo-peep's dream. (Children's dreams are a vast and fascinating topic, which I have largely ignored in this book, for two reasons. First, recording a person's dreams is a form of invasion of privacy to which a child might not be in a position to give informed consent. Second, if the child is not him- or herself capable of offering a dream interpretation, it seems unfair and misleading to offer one from an adult perspective, which the child might not be in a position to accept or even understand.)

Some wish-fulfilment dreams are transparent, and many have their origins in the immediate circumstances of waking life. To take a couple of examples from Freud, if I went to bed thirsty and dreamed of drinking a long, cool glass of water, my dream would express the fulfilment of a wish. Similarly, someone who had been much cut off from company might dream of attending a glittering party. Or, as slightly more emotionally charged examples, a woman who wanted to become pregnant might dream she was pregnant – in such dreams the pregnancy might be represented tangentially, but still in an easily interpretable manner. Similarly, a woman who was pregnant, but reluctantly so, might dream that she was not pregnant; for example she might dream that she had her period as usual.

We talked in Chapter 1 about similarities (and differences) in beliefs about dreams held by the ancient Greeks and by Freud. It seems fitting to examine as our case study one of literature's most famous examples of a wish-fulfilment dream, which happens to come from ancient Greece.

Case study: Penelope, the geese and the eagle

Listen:
>   interpret me this dream: From a water's edge
>   twenty fat geese have come to feed on grain
>   beside my house. And I delight to see them.
>   But now a mountain eagle with great wings
>   and crooked beak storms in to break their necks
>   and strew their bodies here. Away he soars into the bright sky; and
>   I cry aloud –
>   all this in a dream – I wail and round me gather softly braided Akhaian
>   women mourning
>   because the eagle killed my geese.
> Then down
>   out of the sky he drops to a cornice beam
>   and with mortal voice telling me not to weep.
>   'Be glad,' says he, 'renowned Ikários' daughter:
>   here is no dream but something real as day,
>   something about to happen. All those geese were suitors, and the bird was I.
> See now,
>   I am no eagle but your lord come back
>   to bring inglorious death upon them all!'
>   As he said this, my honeyed slumber left me.
>   Peering through half-shut eyes, I saw the geese
>   in hall, still feeding at the self-same trough.
>
>   Homer, *Odyssey*, Book 19, translated by Robert Fitzgerald

Here we have an ancient wish-fulfilment dream that speaks as clearly to modern readers as it did to Homer's first audiences. Penelope was the faithful wife of the hero Odysseus who had gone to the Trojan War to fight for the Greeks. The war lasted ten years and Odysseus took a further ten years to get home. During all that time faithful Penelope waited patiently for the return of her husband, resisting the advances of suitors who flocked to seek her hand. She recounts this dream to Odysseus himself who has just arrived home, although his wife does not recognize him (the goddess Athena has bemused her). She has decided that she will, the next day, impose an archery test on the many suitors and will marry the winner. In the course of the story Odysseus will slay the suitors with the bow and reveal himself to Penelope.

The geese in this dream represent Penelope's suitors, come to eat Odysseus' grain (i.e. live off Odysseus' wealth and take his wife). The eagle represents Odysseus himself. In waking life Penelope longs for her husband, the eagle, to return and rid her of the troublesome suitors, the geese.

In the dream, Penelope is crying over the death of her geese, when the eagle suddenly speaks and reveals himself to be her husband, represented symbolically. Since in waking life Penelope wants to be rid of her suitors, it might seem strange, at first sight, both that Penelope cries over the death of her dream geese, and that in the dream she delighted to see them still alive. Perhaps this is, in fact, a confession on Penelope's part that she has become accustomed to having her suitors around?

But that need not be the only explanation. Inversions of waking feeling are common in dreams; you may have experienced this phenomenon yourself. Perhaps inversion is a way for Penelope to express how much she loathes the suitors. (See the introductory notes on 'Contraries and inversions' in Part two for more on inversions of feeling. The example, given earlier, of a reluctantly pregnant woman dreaming she has her period is another example of inversion.)

In waking life Odysseus, unrecognized by Penelope, now points out the true interpretation of the dream: death to the suitors, sure death too. Not one escapes (Odysseus') doom. Perhaps influenced by the fact that her flesh-and-blood geese were still alive when she woke up, Penelope refuses to accept this and dismisses her dream as mere confusion, a cobweb.

Harnessing the power of your wish-fulfilment dreams

Given its place in the great unfolding drama, Penelope could not be allowed to recognize the true significance of her dream – or to recognize Odysseus, for that matter! But your life does not need to conform to narrative rules. Untangling the meaning of your wish-fulfilment dreams will help you to acknowledge and accept possibly long-suppressed desires and aspects of your personality you do not normally allow yourself to contemplate. Here are some questions to ask yourself if you want to harness the power of your wish-fulfilment dreams for maximum positive effect:

▶ **If the need or desire captured by my dream has taken a struggle to bring to consciousness, why is that so?**

How do you feel about this aspect of your psychological make-up?

▶ **What, if anything, can I do in waking life to change my wish into actuality?**

Is this something you could do alone, or will you need to act co-operatively with others to bring it about?

▶ **How do I feel about sharing details of what my dreams reveal with those closest to me?**

If you want to tell others, think in advance about how you will do so, and what their reactions are likely to be. Is your desire something you feel they would understand, or would they be unsympathetic? How would you feel about an unsupportive reaction from others?

▶ **How do wishes expressed in my dreams relate to consciously acknowledged wishes I am already familiar with and have acted to bring about?**

Do new wishes supersede or complement old ones?

▶ **Is there anything about my wishes, needs or desires that suggests they should remain in the realm of wishes?**

Do they involve anything normally subject to social constraint for good reason? Or anything illegal? Some acts are exciting only so long as they are not put into practice.

▶ **Would fulfilling my wish do me harm?**

For example, if it involved submitting to your desire to smoke, or to drink to excess, or to engage in dangerous sexual activities, you will need to resist such impulses.

▶ **Can I prioritize my wishes and desires?**

If you can prioritize, you will be able to focus your energies on achieving those most important to you, rather than dissipating your energies chasing several dreams at once.

Food for thought: Waking dreams

We commonly speak of our most longed-for desires, especially those which seem difficult or impossible to fulfil, as dreams. In this sense you might say you have a dream of giving up work and moving to the Caribbean, or of moving to the country and starting a little teashop, or becoming a full-time environmental activist. Whatever your waking dream, it is almost certain that somebody, somewhere has achieved it. And what others have done, you can do too! If you have a waking dream, research ways to make it become reality. Perhaps you could start at your local library and read up all you can about your chosen lifestyle and how to achieve it. Or, if you have access to the Internet, get surfing! You will be able to contact like-minded people through chat rooms and email. Draw up an action plan for achieving your waking dream. You could structure it something like this:

Description of my dream – identify your dream as accurately as possible – pin it down. If you want to open a teashop, where do you want this to be? Do you want to run it on your own or with a friend? Would you do all the baking yourself or buy in supplies? If you are not clear about the precise detail of your dream, you will find it difficult to bring about.

My priorities – if you cannot express your priorities, you will find it difficult to act with sufficient focus to bring your dream about.

Obstacles to my progress – if you anticipate obstacles, you will more easily be able to overcome them.

My timescale – this can be several years. However long it is, ensuring that you do have some time limits will give a certain urgency to your project and help keep you motivated.

My progress – build in some mechanisms for checking how far you have come to achieving your end. This could be a diary, a wall chart, the number of chapters of your novel you have finished, or whatever. If you have no means of reviewing progress, you will never know how close you are to achieving your waking dream.

My motivation – remind yourself why you are doing what you are doing. Regularly check that you still endorse this dream or plan – perhaps your values have changed since you started? Dreams change and evolve as you do.

Divination through dreams

In this chapter you will learn:

▶ *about the important role of dreams in divination*
▶ *about divining the past, the present and the future*
▶ *about divination and responsibility to yourself and others.*

Joseph said to Pharaoh, 'Pharaoh's dreams are both the
same... The seven good cows are seven years, and the seven
good ears of grain are seven years – it is all one dream. The
seven lean and gaunt cows that come after them are seven
years, and so also are the seven empty ears of grain blighted
by the east wind... There are to be seven years of bumper
harvests throughout Egypt. After that will come seven
years of famine; so that the great harvests in Egypt will be
forgotten, and famine will ruin the country. The good years
will leave no trace in the land because of the famine that
follows, for it will be very severe.'

Genesis 41, *Revised English Bible*

What is divination through dreams?

Joseph's revelation of the hidden meaning of Pharaoh's dream is
perhaps the most famous example of dream interpretation in all
history. Joseph, an Israelite, had been sold into slavery in Egypt.
He ended up in prison where he acted as a dream interpreter
for other prisoners. One of these was Pharaoh's butler – Joseph
accurately interpreted that one of his dreams showed the butler
was about to be released. A couple of years later Pharaoh began
to have the disturbing dreams of cattle and grain. The butler
remembered Joseph, who was brought before Pharaoh and not
only offered the famous interpretation, but also proposed a
sound economic plan for dealing with the coming crisis – corn
would be collected in the good years, for distribution when
the crops failed. Joseph was put in charge of the scheme for
famine control, became Pharaoh's chief minister and married
the daughter of an Egyptian priest. By the time the famine
duly arrived, Joseph was a wealthy man of great economic and
political power. This story has inspired human imagination
down the ages – right up to the present day, when it formed
the basis for the smash-hit musical *Joseph and the Amazing
Technicolor Dreamcoat*.

Before moving on, it should be pointed out that Joseph
was acting as a dream interpreter for another person – not
something recommended in this book, where the key message

is that your own interpretations of your dreams are the ones that carry significance. Joseph was able to interpret Pharaoh's dreams because the symbols in them (the cows, the grain) had objective, God-given meanings. As we have mentioned elsewhere, symbols do sometimes have *objective* meanings, as here, and also, for example, in the codified systems of representation used by artists in the past. Unlike these special cases, the symbols occurring in your dreams have *subjective* meaning – they are for your mind's eye only, as it were.

Joseph's prediction of the famine is an example of how dreams can be used for divination. People often use the word 'divination' to mean prediction, although it can have a wider meaning. Divination can mean to discover something by inspiration or intuition, rather than through observation or reports of other people's observations. In this sense, we can talk about divination of the past and divination of the present. Dreams can offer divinatory insight into all three phases of time.

Dreams and divination of the past

We have already seen how dreams can supply information about the past. In Chapter 2, India explained how:

▶ she dreamed about her Auntie Sue in a shoe shop, only to learn later that her aunt had once run such a shop

▶ while living in Paris, she had a recurring dream of a battle with an historical setting; she later learned that the house where she was living had been built on the site of a battle that had taken place 200 years previously

India also reports an occasion, not mentioned in Chapter 2, when she had a vivid dream that a dairy maid appeared in her bedroom, only to learn later that the house where she was staying had once been a dairy.

People who accept reincarnation as a possibility often argue that dreams can provide a means of bringing to consciousness memories from previous incarnations. It is sometimes suggested that dreams about one's previous lives have three key features:

1 **They are set in the past** – a fairly obvious requirement.

2 **The dreamer him- or herself is not seen in the dream;** rather, the dream unfolds from the perspective of an unobserved person. This is how we experience waking life – we do not literally see ourselves living our lives, but all of life is experienced from our own unique perspective. It is argued that, if this pattern occurs in dreams, it is at least suggestive that the perspective of the unseen character is the perspective of the dreamer in a previous life.

3 **The dreams recur,** although not with precisely the same details each time they are dreamed. For example, the dreamer may have recurring dreams about life as a French monk in the twelfth century. Each dream might offer different insights into being a twelfth-century French monk – dreams of attending Mass, dining with fellow brethren, working at an illuminated manuscript, or whatever.

In addition, reincarnation dreams may be accompanied by:

▶ **detailed and recurring waking visions** – in our example, the dreamer who dreamed of the French monk might get recurring waking visions of a monastery or the interior of a church

▶ **déjà vu** – a powerful awareness of familiarity in supposedly unfamiliar surroundings or circumstances; in our example a ruined monastery might trigger such a feeling.

Harnessing the power of your dreams about the past

When you dream of the past you have access to memories, or quasi-memories, or memory traces that affect you now. If these are disturbing or negative (they may be positive – in which case, great!) and you can confront them and deal with them, then you can help yourself come to terms with deep-rooted problems and to move on – whatever it was that happened,

happened. But the past is gone and now it is time to bear in mind the following:

▶ By coming to an understanding of the meanings of your dreams about the past, you will be empowered to change those meanings for yourself and to make the meanings positive. For example, if you frequently dream of a man in an historical setting who is both violent and drunken, and you come to understand this as a memory trace from a past life, you could interpret its impact on the present and future in various ways – as a reason to aim for the top yourself, as there is only one way to go from the scenario of the dream, or as a prediction that you will yourself fall into drunkenness and violence.

▶ Dreams of the past, especially of past lives, can carry information and advice about persistent, destructive patterns of behaviour, perhaps in relationships. Dreams of the past could help the dreamer come to understand why he or she is locked into a pattern of choosing abusive partners or of entering relationships expecting them to end. Such dreams might also help explain why the dreamer suffers from a pattern involving having and losing in all spheres of life.

▶ Interpreting dreams of the past can help us confront, understand and conquer phobias, such as fear of flying or fear of drowning. They can also help with goal orientation and setting priorities.

Dreams and divination of the present

Every human emotion, experience, quality, possibility and physical state can be reflected in dreams. The subconscious has the power to assimilate information in a way we cannot comprehend with our conscious minds. In dreams, this power can be brought to bear on currently hidden problems in our lives. For example, the first hint that one's partner is having an affair might come through a dream. Or a parent might receive dream warnings that his or her teenage child has started experimenting with drugs.

Dreams can often provide information about the current state of the body – our subconscious has the power to detect changes long before outward signs or symptoms appear. Sometimes this power is itself represented graphically in dreams. Louise, whom we met in Chapters 3 and 5, reports a recurring dream where she is reduced to minuscule size and is walking around the interior of her own body. Surely this is a symbol of her subconscious in its role of watchful guard?

Many women report that they dream of being pregnant before they have taken a (positive) pregnancy test – I have twice had this experience. Or dreams may convey warnings of illness or physical weakness. For example, Bob, an apparently healthy man in his mid-thirties, had recurring dreams of breathing difficulties and restrictions around his chest. After several months he took this warning seriously and had a full medical check-up. This revealed that he had a very high cholesterol level and that smoking was having a detrimental effect on his lung capacity and efficiency. Bob was frightened enough to make long-resisted changes to his diet and lifestyle. Thus his dreams had a beneficial effect, helping Bob to take tough decisions and lower some controllable risks for heart disease.

As we mentioned in Chapter 1, and will discuss again in Chapter 10, the Ancients paid close attention to what their dreams told them about their health. They believed that dreams could suggest diagnoses, prognoses and cures for illness. In our modern era, we tend to ignore dream messages about our bodies. Out of curiosity, I asked a friend who is a doctor whether his patients ever mentioned their dreams to him. The answer was no – they told him their fears, anxieties and problems, but not their dreams. Perhaps we would all be healthier, and need to consult doctors less, if we tried to adopt the ancient perspective on dreams. (I am not suggesting you burden your hugely overworked family doctor with detailed accounts of all your dreams, rather, simply, that you remain alert to messages they might convey about your health!)

Many folk tales and fairy tales attest to the importance of divinatory dreams about the present. For example, in the fairy tale *Beauty and the Beast*, the heroine, Beauty finds herself left alone in a castle with a beast:

> She went to her bedroom and cried herself to sleep. She dreamed that a handsome prince came to her and said, 'Don't be unhappy Beauty. You will be rewarded for your goodness. Do not leave me.'

Her dream is telling her that the Beast is really a prince, although she is not yet in a position to recognize this. When this time finally comes, she is back with her family and has a second divinatory dream about the present:

> In it she saw the Beast dying. She woke and ran to her father. 'I must return at once,' she told him. 'The poor Beast is dying because I have stayed too long.'

Beauty returns to the Beast and kisses him, and he, of course, transforms into the handsome prince of her dreams – a tale of sexual politics and the redemptive power of love for the very young! (Quotes are taken from the Oyster Books version of this story, published by Hodder.)

Another type of dream that can be regarded as providing divinatory knowledge of the present is the inspirational dream (i.e. a dream containing the solution to a problem currently exercising your mind). One of the most famous examples of this sort of dream concerns the discovery of the ring-like structure of benzene. This structure was discovered by a German chemist called Friedrich August Kekulé in the middle of the nineteenth century. One day, while working on the problem of the structure of benzene, Kekulé sat staring into the fire, fell asleep and dreamed the flames formed a serpent swallowing its own tail – this suggested the ring structure to him.

Perhaps Kekulé was not fully asleep, but in the highly creative state between waking and sleeping known as hypnogogia. This is a time, or condition, of heightened sensitivity to visions, ideas and creative insights of all sorts. Or perhaps Kekulé was merely gazing into the fire – the point is that non-rational forces guided him to a rational answer to a problem.

Harnessing the power of your dreams about the present

The best way to harness the power of dreams about the present is to listen to them. Ask yourself:

▶ **Is your dream telling you something about your body?**

If so, act on it! Take a test, see your doctor, change your diet, take up exercise, try to quit smoking ... or whatever.

▶ **Is your dream telling you something negative about your marriage or your family?**

If so, think about how you will discover whether your dream is accurate and make a plan for dealing with any possible repercussions. Think about how you will raise this issue with your partner or children, and also about the most desirable outcome for all concerned. Do not rush into hasty speech or action, but remember that knowledge gives you a power that you can use for the good. (Of course, your dreams can convey joyful as well as gloomy information.)

▶ **Are your dreams telling you something about the current state of your emotions or your psyche?**

If so, why does it require your dreams to make this plain to you? Do you resist acknowledging your state in waking life? If so, why? What are you scared to confront? How can your new insight help you fulfil your ambitions, meet your needs or maximize your potential?

▶ **Are your dreams offering you a flash of insight into some seemingly intractable problem?**

If so, be prepared to follow the insight to its ultimate conclusion.

Dreams and divination of the future

As we already mentioned, when people talk about using dreams for divination, they most often have in mind using dreams for prediction – so-called prophetic dreams, ones that foretell future events. Prophetic dreams can be subdivided in various ways:

- **Neutral precognitive** – dreams simply letting you know that this or that relatively unimportant event will probably happen, or not.

- **Joyous precognitive** – dreams foretelling some happy event, such as a marriage or a promotion. Many people report romantic precognitive dreams featuring their future spouse. Person A dreams of meeting person B in a specific setting and a specific context. Later, the meeting occurs in waking life and A and B become deeply involved with each other.

- **Gambling** – dreams conveying the name of the winner, or winning team, in sporting events, enabling the dreamer to lay a successful bet. For example, the dreamer may dream that they are reading the racing results in the next day's evening paper, and will awake with the names of the horses placed first and second. Or they may dream they are listening to racing commentary on the radio and similarly gain information about the winners. Many people select their lottery ticket numbers according to hints from their dreams – it would be interesting to find out how many of these people are successful, although I know of no research on the subject. Some investors use information supplied by their dreams when making investment choices, a form of financial gambling.

- **Warning** – since humans have a natural tendency to focus on the negative, perhaps the most common type of prophetic dream, and certainly the most frequently reported, is the warning. India has already shared such a dream with us – she dreamed that her Auntie Sue was going to die, several months before the event. Similarly, Tamara, another high-flying career woman, has four times dreamed of already dead people close to still-living people who were themselves about to die (e.g. she dreamed of her living aunt's dead husband on the night her aunt unexpectedly died). She is now very worried about such dreams. Impending death is not the only subject of warning dreams; natural disasters often feature, as do crashes, bombings, illness, etc. In ancient times, many warning dreams concerned the path of war or the outcome of battles.

▶ **Advisory** – the dream may offer straightforward advice: do this, or do that. The power of the dream is often reinforced by the identity of the dream messenger. This is often someone of great importance in the dreamer's life – a parent, child, lover, or whoever. Or it could be an archetypal child, lover, wise old man, etc. In some cultures people frequently report divine dream messengers. In Chapter 1 we had the example of Zeus sending a dream to Agamemnon (here the advice was malicious). Modern counterparts might be advisory dreams where the dream messenger was a figure of great religious significance – such as a priest or rabbi.

▶ **Reincarnational** – dreams hinting at future lives. These dreams have the same features as reincarnational dreams of the past – except that they are set in the future. Like reincarnational dreams of the past, they are frequently accompanied by recurrent waking visions, but here the feeling of precognition replaces déjà vu. Precognition is the unexplained acquisition of knowledge about events that lie in the relatively near future (it has to be relatively near if you are to test the accuracy of your precognitive ability). Those who accept the notion of reincarnation think we will have lives in the future as well in the past, and that dreams can somehow bring anticipations of what these lives might hold to consciousness during our current life. The notion of anticipating future lives carries some difficulties because we ordinarily think of time travelling in a straight line, forwards. But perhaps time is not like a line, but like a circle or a spiral. Or perhaps, if time is a line, it can run backwards. Those who admit such possibilities may classify some of their dreams as being of future lives.

Warning or anxiety?

It is important to try to distinguish between genuine warning dreams and disguised anxiety dreams. For example, I frequently dream about air crashes. I do not interpret these as predictions, but as expressions of my anxiety about flying.

Harnessing the power of your dreams about the future

Dreams of the future are the easiest of the divinatory dreams to act upon:

► If you are lucky enough, or intuitive enough, to have a track record of using dreams successfully in gambling, then trust information supplied by your dreams, and place those bets. Or buy or sell those shares, subject to studying market conditions and taking all normal precautions.

► If, in the past, your dreams have conveyed accurate warnings about the future, then do not ignore other such warnings, as and when they occur.

► Take the advice offered in your dreams seriously, especially when conveyed by a powerful figure in your life.

► Never be afraid to trust the insights and inspiration conveyed by your dreams – remember, the structure of benzene might have remained mysterious for many years if Kekulé had not trusted his dreams. Such inspiration could apply to the future as well as to the present.

► Think about how and why the style in which you live now might affect any future lives you might possibly live.

Food for thought: Dream predictions and responsibility

No dream of the future ever deals in certainty. Such dreams deal in probability or likelihood – they tell us that something is more or less likely to happen, not that it will or will not happen. Dreams do not convey information about some immovable fate or destiny, but offer hints, warnings and suggestions about various paths open to you at a given time and point in your life. Your dreams do not license you to abdicate responsibility for your own actions or your own future. If or when you decide to act on information supplied in dreams, you act under your own free will. You are responsible for the choices you make and the consequences of those choices.

Nightmares

In this chapter you will learn:

▶ *how to reduce the terror of nightmares*
▶ *to consider some of the different causes of nightmares*
▶ *some tips for dealing with insomnia.*

Isabel once was asleep in bed
When a horrible dream crawled into her head.
It was worse than a dinosaur, worse than a shark,
Worse than an octopus oozing in the dark.
'Boo!' said the dream, with a dreadful grin,
'I'm going to scare you out of your skin!'

Ogden Nash (1902–71), *The Adventures of Isabel*

What are nightmares?

The word 'nightmare' is derived from an Anglo-Saxon word (*mære*) used to describe an evil spirit supposed to descend on sleeping persons, intent on sexual intercourse, or a monster seeming to suffocate the sleeper. It is easy to see how this led to the modern sense of an intensely vivid, oppressive, paralysing, or fantastically horrible dream.

The historical connection between demons intent on sex and nightmares does not mean that nightmares are invariably sexual; indeed, some evidence suggests that they are relatively seldom sexual in content, although victims of incest or rape, for example, may review these awful experiences in their dreams. Most often, nightmares are a form of anxiety dream, connected with some prior event of a traumatic nature, such as a physical attack, an accident, imprisonment, etc. Or nightmares may have biological causes (e.g. they may be experienced during withdrawal of sleeping tablets). Or they may be prompted by guilt feelings that the dreamer is unable to deal with, or even to acknowledge, in waking life. Some nightmares are commonly reported (e.g. those featuring being naked in a public place). Nightmares often repeatedly recur. Frequently they feature chase and pursuit. (See the relevant chapters for anxiety dreams, recurring dreams and chase dreams. Sexual dreams are dealt with in Chapter 6.)

Nightmares should be distinguished from night terrors. Unlike nightmares, night terrors are accompanied by powerful physiological effects – heart and respiratory rates shoot up, and there is often sweating and sometimes loud screaming. The content of night terrors is often a conviction of suffocation, choking or entrapment. Nightmares, like all dreams, occur during REM sleep; night terrors occur during deep, non-REM sleep. Both are frequently experienced by children.

Childhood or adolescent nightmares may be remembered well into adult life. For instance, one correspondent in her mid-thirties reports that one of her most vivid and terrifying dreams occurred when she was 14 or 15 years old. She dreamed of a man sitting at an office desk. All she could really see was his hand, which was illuminated by an angle-poise lamp. The finger was pointing and running down a long list of names, as in a telephone directory. In her dream the woman knew that the historical period was the Second World War, that this man was a Nazi officer, and that she was Jewish. He was searching for her own name. The woman woke up in terror and has never forgotten the dream. The dreamer's mother is Jewish and, although she was brought up in almost complete ignorance of Jewish ritual, religion and law, as a child she frequently saw pictures of family members who had died in concentration camps. Undoubtedly this influenced her dream.

Case studies: David and Marion

We are going to look at two nightmares that, in each case, the dreamer came to understand as being prompted by unresolved guilt.

David's dreams

David is a high-flying executive working for a large multinational company. Like many others, his organization undertook sweeping restructuring and downsizing during a period of economic difficulty. Over a three-month period it fell to David to make more than 20 staff redundant. The guilt and stress accompanying this process soon began to filter into David's dreams. (It should not be forgotten, nor did David forget, that however miserable he felt, the people he made redundant were far more deserving of sympathy than he was himself.)

David did not usually remember many of his dreams, or have an especially vivid dream life. But after the round of redundancies, he would frequently dream that the disembodied head of one or other of the people he had fired was following him around at the office. He would try to push the heads away, but his hand would pass right through them, as through a ghost. The heads never spoke, but they stared fixedly at him. This made it impossible for him to concentrate on his dream activities, which mirrored his daily activities – chairing meetings, seeing clients, etc. In his dreams colleagues would ask him why he seemed so distracted, and he would say 'Can't you see so-and-so is following me around?' But the heads were invisible to all but him. In his dreams his weird behaviour at work caused his colleagues to shun him, although in waking life he remained popular at work, despite his recent firings. David would wake up exhausted, anxious and most unwilling to go into the office. When he got there he felt demotivated and depressed. The dreams went on for some months, but eased as news filtered through that his former staff were getting new jobs – he even saw one or two of them socially.

Marion's dreams

Marion is in her mid-thirties, married with a daughter aged ten years old. She frequently has nightmares that her child is being bullied at school, although her own observations and repeated questioning, both of her daughter and her daughter's teachers, have produced no evidence whatsoever that this is actually going on, and her daughter is well adjusted, popular and academically able.

In the dreams, her daughter is most often standing alone in a circle of girls who are silently staring at her. Or else her daughter is being bossed around and bullied with non-specific threats of punishment – 'Do this, or do that, or we will do this or that to you!' The things she is being asked to do are always either dangerous or of the sort to get her into trouble. Marion's daughter never resists these requests, or opposes the other girls in any way, but is nevertheless punished by banishment from the group. In the dreams, Marion knows what is going on but has no idea how to help her daughter, or what to do, and this confusion and sense of powerlessness make her deeply unhappy and anxious. She frequently wakes up feeling panicky.

It might be natural to interpret such dreams as straightforward expressions of an understandable anxiety – after all, mothers do worry that their children might be bullied. But Marion does not interpret them this way. Rather she thinks they are a way of forcing her to acknowledge the meanness of some of her own behaviour at school. She went to an all-girls' school and in her class there was a fat girl who was quite plain and not particularly clever. She was an easy target for the other girls and soon became the butt of the entire class's jokes, pranks and casual cruelties. Things got so bad that their class teacher had to make an excuse to send the target girl out of the room, so she could lecture the rest of them about the unacceptable nature of their behaviour. This only made things worse – the teasing intensified, but became more secretive. Marion always felt bad about what was going on, but never spoke up and never offered the other girl friendship, out of concern that if she did either of these things she, too, would become the object of the class's derision.

Marion feels that her current nightmares about her daughter are her subconscious's way of forcing her to confront and deal with long-suppressed guilt over her childhood behaviour. There is little she can now do to make amends to the girl concerned, since they lost touch many years ago. But she does talk to her daughter about the horrors of bullying and about trying to resist group pressures and herd instincts – something that she is now, in her adult life, careful to do.

Harnessing the power of your nightmares

Frightening and ghastly as nightmares are, Marion's case clearly shows their potential power to help you bring about positive changes in your psyche. Marion began to come to terms with an old misdemeanour and previously suppressed guilt by helping her daughter avoid her own mistakes, and by thinking about the role of peer pressure in her adult life. As well as helping you come to terms with guilt, here are some of the other potential benefits of nightmares:

▶ Prophetic nightmares can help you to avoid whatever scenario they depict, by taking heed and taking action *now*. The old saying has it that forewarned is forearmed. Use the prophetic insights of your nightmares to prepare you to face, avoid and overcome future problems. (See Chapter 8 for a full discussion of prophetic dreams.)

▶ If horrible events from your past are depicted in your nightmares, try to understand them as offering you a chance to review (not relive) those events, and as a chance to understand why what happened did happen. Your nightmares can perhaps help you to change the negative meanings of awful events into less negative, neutral or even positive meanings. If you are truly haunted by images and

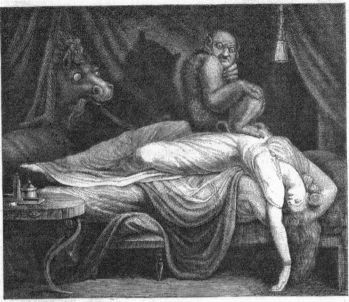

THE NIGHTMARE.

Figure 9.1 An engraving after Henry Fuseli's famous painting *The Nightmare* (1781). The painting evokes the folk etymology of 'nightmare' from the term for a female horse, although in reality *mare* was an Old English word for a demon.

memories of bad things in your past, you might want to seek the help of a suitably qualified therapist or counsellor. Your family doctor should be able to offer you initial advice or introduce you to a counselling service.

▶ Nightmares can help you focus on problems currently manifesting in your life, and hence give you the opportunity to take action to avoid those problems, or lessen their effects. For example, if you regularly have nightmares about work, or about commuting, could you make changes in your working patterns, or your daily routine, to lessen the stress? If you have nightmares about family situations, could you similarly take action?

▶ If your nightmares are rooted in phobias – fear of flying, of spiders, of drowning, of being trapped in a small space, etc. – could you consider tackling your phobia with the help of a skilled professional? Again, your family doctor might be able to help. Or hypnotherapy might help, but you need to be careful when choosing a hypnotherapist, as you put yourself completely in his or her power. Word of mouth is a good recommendation; it is also a positive sign if he or she is a member of a reputable governing body.

▶ If your nightmares started after you began taking a particular medication, talk to your doctor about whether the drugs could be a cause. Beware, too, of over-the-counter remedies. I suffered vivid, detailed nightmares after taking a particular type of over-the-counter remedy for jet lag, which worked by regulating body hormones implicated in maintaining the normal sleep–waking biorhythm. If you have nightmares after eating or drinking a particular type of food or drink, avoid it! Cheese and red wine are often cited as culprits.

Remember, while you sleep you are vulnerable. On waking, you – with all your fantastic and amazing mental capabilities – are stronger than any nightmare. We started this chapter with a quotation from Ogden Nash's *The Adventures of Isabel*. This tells the story of a bold little girl who overcomes all sorts of childhood terrors – a bear, a witch, a giant, etc. After describing Isabel's nightmare the poem continues:

Isabel, Isabel, didn't worry
Isabel didn't scream or scurry.
Isabel had a clever scheme:
She just woke up and fooled that dream.

Isabel had the waking courage to say boo to her nightmares and scare them away – you have that courage, too.

Dream catchers

If you regularly suffer from nightmares, it might be worth investing in a Native American dream catcher – widely available in new age shops. These decorative hangings for the bedroom feature a large central net that Native Americans used to represent the web of the world. According to traditional belief, these nets, or webs, would catch bad dreams before they could disturb the sleeper.

Food for thought: Dealing with insomnia

Insomnia – difficulty in sleeping or disturbance in the normal sleep pattern – is common. Nightmares need not be linked to insomnia, but some people are regularly woken by bad dreams. If you do suffer from insomnia, there are several things you can do to help yourself get a good night's sleep:

✳ Often **physical factors** are to blame for disturbed sleep – eating too late, a room that is too hot or too cold, noise, drafts, etc. Try to identify and eliminate any such factors. Make a routine for going to bed: a bath, a hot drink, an undemanding book to read (nothing so exciting that you will want to stay up until it is finished!). Avoid any foods you know to cause you nightmares.

✳ **Worry** is the other main cause of insomnia – and the one most likely to feed into your nightmares. If you worry about time management, at work or at home, get up and write an action plan of things to do the next day, rather than let worry interfere with your sleep and, perhaps, your dreams. If you worry over relationships, try getting up and writing down what is troubling you. If you worry over things you cannot name, get up and read a book, or do something useful, until you feel able to return to bed, and to sleep.

✳ Remember that **sex is an excellent hypnotic** – it will help put you to sleep!

✳ **Do not drink alcohol** prior to retiring; it will help you fall asleep, but the effect can be short lived and you might find yourself waking up early or thirsty.

✳ Insomnia can be a feature of **depression**. If you have other features of depression, such as poor concentration, inability to enjoy things, gloom, lack of libido or excess drinking, talk to your family doctor.

✳ Many **complementary therapies** offer help for insomnia. Herbal tea bags containing mixtures of herbs to help you sleep are widely available. Lavender essential oil is helpful, and Bach Flower Remedies can help relieve psychological upsets leading to disturbed sleep. Many homoeopathic remedies can help. Consult the therapist of your choice for detailed advice.

✳ **Never take sleeping pills without first consulting your family doctor**. Tolerance soon develops (the dosage has to be raised for the same effect), addiction is likely, and withdrawal problems are a real possibility. Your doctor will probably regard sleeping pills as a last resort and will not prescribe them for more than a short time.

Dream incubation

In this chapter you will learn:

▶ *how to use the power of dreams in a variety of contexts*

▶ *about the link between dreams and positive affirmation*

▶ *some of the connections between dreams and superstition.*

Full of gratitude, I departed cured.

Recipient of Asclepius' dream-conveyed wisdom

What is dream incubation?

To incubate is to bring forth, or to cause development of something. Dream incubation involves actively generating a sought dream to help to achieve various ends, including:

▶ solving a specific problem

▶ reaching a decision

▶ overcoming an emotional or psychic obstacle to self-fulfilment

▶ generating ideas

▶ promoting physical healing

▶ stimulating creative thought.

Members of various cultures have, throughout history, sought to develop and master methods of dream incubation. Some of the earliest records are from Egypt and refer to practices in use in about 1500 BCE. Ancient methods were often focused on making contact with ghosts or gods.

Not all ancient methods would be considered either safe or sensible in the West today. Some of the methods I would certainly not recommend include self-flagellation, fasting, sleep deprivation and even self-mutilation. One Native American practice involved lopping off a finger joint in the hope of promoting a sought dream. This practice was explained as an appeasement of the god, whose dream apparition was desired, by an act that symbolized self-castration. In the ancient world, some men claimed to be able to sell a dreamer any dream he or she desired, for a small fee. If anyone claimed to be able to do this today, it would seem wise to treat them with extreme caution.

Some of the ancient methods that could be adapted to modern life are listed below:

▶ **Isolation, perhaps accompanied by meditation, contemplation or prayer** – withdrawal to a sacred place in search of visionary wisdom features in many legends.

The modern version might be to take a weekend retreat, or simply to tell all your friends, colleagues and family that you will be unavailable for a few days.

► **Sleeping on the skin of a sacred animal** – in modern life, this could be adapted to sleeping in sight of a picture of an animal that has personal meaning for you. This could be an animal you especially love, your Chinese horoscope animal (which you will be able to find with the help of any book on Chinese astrology), or your Native American totem (which you will be able to find from books on Native American spirituality). The idea is that your dreams should be infused by the energies, potentialities and abilities of your chosen animal.

► **Sleeping in contact with a sacred object** – the modern equivalent might be sleeping in contact with a healing crystal, or, if you seek a dream about a specific person, perhaps a dead person, sleeping in contact with an object that belongs, or once belonged, to that person. If you want to dream about a place, try sleeping in contact with something taken from that place, a map showing its location, or a picture in which it is featured.

► **Sleeping in a holy place** – in the ancient world, sleeping in a holy place was sometimes used to promote dreams of the dead, but most often for medical purposes. As we mentioned in Chapter 1, the cult of Asclepius was important in Greece. Sick people came to sleep in Asclepius' temple precincts in the hope that the god would reveal his will in their dreams and either effect an immediate cure, perhaps by surgery performed while they slept, or reveal which measures or remedies they should try. In the modern world, sleeping in a holy place might translate into preparing your sleeping quarters using particular rituals that you have developed in accordance with your own personality, preferences and desires. Perhaps you could paint your bedroom a particular colour, place particular images about the room, fall asleep to a favourite piece of music, or burn a particular type of incense. Or you could try camping in particularly beautiful, or significant, surroundings. Technically, sleeping in a holy place is the only method that should be called incubation, but I have widened the definition, as is now common.

Figure 10.1 The remains of a temple of Asclepius. In the Classical world, people would sleep in temple precincts in the hope of deliberately incubating revelatory dreams.

▶ Sleeping with a branch of laurel under your pillow – something recommended in ancient dreambooks and a practice that survived in Europe until relatively recently. As well as laurel, you could try a bunch of herbs, or a handkerchief on which you have placed a few drops of essential oil.

Psychic suggestion, positive affirmation and visualization

Perhaps the three most practical and accessible techniques for promoting a sought dream nowadays are psychic suggestion, positive affirmation and visualization.

PSYCHIC SUGGESTION

By this I mean immersing yourself in the hours leading up to bedtime in material relating to whatever it is you wish to dream about. For example, should you wish to dream about:

▶ **a particular person:** study photographs of that person, try to hold one of his or her belongings, think about personality and characteristics, try to remember times you spent together.

- ▶ **a particular event:** try to study books, articles or other printed matter related to that event, or ask others to tell you what they remember about it. Old videos or diaries could also contribute information.

- ▶ **a particular place:** try to hold things taken from that place, study any printed material relating to the place, photographs, maps, etc. Try to recall any time you spent there.

- ▶ **money:** try to think about money in a structured way – read the financial pages of the newspapers, hold money, study coins and notes carefully. Jot down a few thoughts about your attitude to money and its role in your life.

- ▶ **health:** think about your health, pamper your body, or study it in a mirror. Look at images of healthy bodies in magazines, browse in a health shop, etc.

- ▶ **a relationship:** read over any love letters you have kept, look at photographs of you and your lover, think about your hopes and fears for the relationship, etc.

It is impossible to give specific advice for every type of dream you might wish to promote, or for every possible type of problem you might wish to tackle in your dreams. The above suggestions are intended for inspiration only, to give you some clues about how you might undertake psychic suggestion.

Whatever you wish to dream about, and whatever the specific method of psychic suggestion you adopt, it is important that you clarify in your own mind precisely what it is you want to achieve from your hoped-for dream. Write down what you hope to learn from the dream, or recite it aloud. This will prime your subconscious to get going on producing creative and helpful insights.

POSITIVE AFFIRMATION
Positive affirmation is a particularly powerful type of psychic suggestion. Positive affirmations are short, upbeat statements that can prod the mind into working in constructive ways. They can be used to help you determine the general subject matter of a dream, or to help focus your mind on finding the solution to a particular problem as you dream.

Positive affirmations should be:

▶ in the first person and should include your own name

▶ in the present tense

▶ short and easy to remember

▶ positively focused on the outcome you want, not negatively focused on the problem (e.g. 'I, Jane, am cool under pressure', not 'I, Jane, must never lose my temper').

Affirmations can be written down, spoken aloud or silently, or recorded on tape. They can be used at any time (e.g. on the bus or in the bath). When you are using them to try to promote a given dream, try to repeat one many times during the day on which you hope to have the dream. Once in bed, repeat the affirmation to yourself to the rhythm of your breathing, as you fall asleep.

Here are some examples of affirmations you could use to promote dreams. As above, it is possible to give only a few examples, to provide general guidelines about how you might proceed, given your unique personality, circumstances and problems.

▶ 'Tonight I, [name], will dream about whether to accept my new job offer.'

▶ 'Tonight I, [name], will dream that I am a confident and strong public speaker.'

▶ 'Tonight I, [name], will dream about overcoming barriers to communication in my relationship.' (Note the positive nature of this statement. As mentioned, do not cast affirmations in negative terms, e.g. do not say: 'I, [name], will dream about what is wrong with my relationship.')

▶ 'Tonight I, [name], will dream about how to balance my monthly budget and become financially organized.'

▶ 'Tonight I, [name], will dream about overcoming my shyness so others can more easily see my vibrant personality.'

▶ 'Tonight I, [name], will dream that my back is pain free for one whole day.'

VISUALIZATION

Visualization is also a form of psychic suggestion. It is a kind of structured daydreaming that can help bring about desired mental states. You can use it as an aid to dream incubation in the following way:

1 Once you are warm and comfortable in bed, and ready for sleep, try to formulate to yourself as clearly as you can the end you wish to achieve in your sought dream – the solution to an intellectual problem, the resolution of financial worries, relationship advice, or whatever.

2 Then picture in your mind how you would behave once this problem is resolved – would you be more relaxed, less anxious, more confident? And how would this change affect your behaviour? Try to be as detailed as you can in your imaginings.

3 Once you have focused on your chosen outcome, let your conscious and subconscious minds do the rest, as you cross the border from wakefulness into sleep.

Traditional methods of promoting dreams

You could try the traditional methods described below, as most are easily adaptable to modern circumstances. But often the core activity was accompanied by special rituals or incantations, not given here. Or else it had to be undertaken at a particular time of year (such as Hallowe'en) to be effective. If you want fuller details of how these superstitions operated, *A Dictionary of Superstitions,* edited by Iona Opie and Moira Tatem and published by Oxford University Press, gives comprehensive coverage.

Food for thought: Superstition and dream incubation

Many superstitions that survived in Europe until relatively recently concern methods of promoting dreams. Most commonly, these seem to have concerned promoting a dream about one's future spouse. Recommended techniques included:

* sleeping with a piece of wedding cake under your pillow
* procuring a shoulder bone of a sheep, pricking it nine times, or making nine holes in it, placing it under your pillow and reciting a version of the following rhyme before retiring: ''Tis not the bone I mean to prick, / But my love's heart I wish to prick; / If he comes not and speaks tonight, / I'll prick and prick till it be light.'
* placing a piece of coal, preferably retrieved from under a plantain plant at noon on Midsummer's Eve, under your pillow at night
* keeping silent while baking a special cake, often made with bizarre ingredients such as soot or urine, then either eating some of the cake or placing it under one's pillow, before retiring
* placing the first egg ever laid by a white hen under one's pillow
* placing nine smooth holly leaves, picked according to special rituals, in a handkerchief, tying nine knots in this, and then placing it under one's pillow
* rubbing the bedposts with lemon peel, previously carried about one's person for a day – preferably under one's armpits
* sticking an onion with nine pins, then reciting a version of the following verse and placing it under one's pillow: 'Good Saint Thomas, do me right, / Send me my true love this night, / In his clothes and his array, / Which he weareth every day.'
* eating very salty food before retiring – in one's dreams one's future spouse would bring one a drink (in an alternative version, if one ate salty food and then dreamed of one's lover offering one water, this was a sign that one would be jilted)
* placing one's shoes in the shape of a letter T at the foot of the bed.

People also sought to promote other types of dream. A diamond placed under the pillow was believed to promote a dream that would reveal whether or not one's partner had been unfaithful. Sometimes people slept with pieces of christening cake under their pillows, to promote dreams about their future children.

Lucid and mutual dreams

In this chapter you will learn:

▶ *about the phenomenon of lucid dreams*
▶ *how two people can participate in one lucid dream*
▶ *how to generate lucid dreams.*

A lord takes his servant, Tarokaja, and goes to Nishinomiya to pray for a wife. Since Tarokaja is also single, both men petition for wives. After reaching the shrine, they pray and fall asleep. When the lord wakes up, he describes a dream in which he was informed he would find a fish hook near the Western gate. If he throws the fish hook into the sea, he will catch a wife. Tarokaja tells the lord he had exactly the same dream.

Tsuri Onna [Fishing for a Wife], a traditional
Japanese tale, often presented in dramatic form

What are lucid dreams?

A lucid dream is one in which the dreamer is consciously aware that he or she is dreaming. The experienced lucid dreamer can consciously manipulate dream content. Almost anything is possible in such dreams – almost anything can be dreamed into becoming reality. Through controlling your dream life, you can change your waking life, and the power of lucid dreams can be harnessed:

- to overcome fears, anxiety and phobias

- for healing and to improve physical health

- to find creative solutions to problems

- as a vehicle for spiritual enlightenment

- for education

- for entertainment.

WHO CAN LEARN TO HAVE LUCID DREAMS?
Stephen LaBerge, one of the foremost researchers of lucid dreaming, argues that this question is analogous to the question 'Who can learn to talk?' Apart from exceptional cases, everyone learns basic proficiency in their own language. A few develop the basic proficiency into an art form and become skilled dramatists, poets or orators. Similarly, LaBerge thinks, everyone should be able to attain a basic proficiency in lucid dreaming, although the Shakespeares of the lucid dreaming world are bound to be few.

LaBerge thinks there are two essentials for learning lucid dreaming: motivation and the ability to recall lucid dreams. Motivation is required because lucid dreaming demands considerable control of attention, and we must be motivated to make the effort.

As this book has stressed, before you undertake any kind of dream work, you must be able to recall your dreams. To achieve dream recall, of whatever type of dream – not just lucid dreams – you must be prepared to keep a dream journal, your own bridge between the worlds of waking and sleeping. Reread Chapter 2 if you need advice on starting and using a dream journal.

One of the functions of a dream journal is to help you become familiar with the quality and style of your dreams. This familiarity will help you to recognize your dreams as dreams, while they are unfolding – the first step on the road to becoming a lucid dreamer. Once you are familiar with the style of your dreams, you can even tell yourself that next time you are dreaming you will recognize that you are dreaming.

TECHNIQUES FOR PROMOTING LUCID DREAMING
Once you are skilled in dream recall, learning to dream lucidly is a two-step process. First you have to learn to recognize that you are dreaming as your dream unfolds, then you have to learn how to exert your will in your dreams (i.e. how to control content).

▶ **1 Recognizing that you are in a dream**

Beyond recording all your dreams so that you become familiar with your dream style, how can you learn to recognize that you are dreaming, as you dream? Successful lucid dreamers report a variety of techniques that can help the novice. The first five on the list are designed to prompt you to think about your state of consciousness, not something we normally do, either when awake or when dreaming. If we reflect on our state of consciousness, then we are more likely to become aware that we are dreaming, as we dream.

▶ **The magic question.** Many people regard 'Am I dreaming?' as a magic question. If asked often enough in waking situations, it will become natural to ask it in your dreams, which raises the possibility that you might be able to give the answer 'yes'.

▶ **Magic question linked to trigger situation.** Try to remember to ask 'Am I dreaming?' every time you perform some routine waking action, such as brushing your teeth or crossing a road. Eventually you will almost certainly dream of the trigger situation. In your dream you will ask the magic question, again leading to the possibility that you can answer 'yes'.

▶ **Magic question linked to observation of the bizarre.** Bizarre things happen in waking life, but they happen far more frequently in dreams. Every time you ask the magic question, look for signs of the bizarre. If you see something strange, you may be able to answer 'yes'. Similarly, if you spot something bizarre, remember to ask the magic question 'Am I dreaming?' Again, you may be able to answer 'yes'.

▶ **Reality checks.** The bizarre may sometimes happen in waking life, but the physically impossible does not. If you begin to suspect that you may be dreaming, try to do something physically impossible, such as flying, walking through a wall or extending your body like a telescope. If you can do something physically impossible, you are dreaming.

▶ **Trigger objects.** Choose some ordinary trigger object – a particular teapot, a particular book – and tell yourself that when you see it in a dream you will know that you are dreaming. Eventually you will almost certainly see your chosen trigger object in a dream, and your mind should prompt you into conscious recognition that you are dreaming.

▶ **Counting.** Try counting: 'I am in a dream 1, I am in a dream 2, I am in a dream 3…' as you fall asleep. This should enable you to maintain conscious awareness during the transition from wakefulness to sleep. At some point in the sequence you should become aware that you are, in fact, dreaming. Counting can be particularly useful for people who experience sleep-onset dreams (hypnogogia). Maintaining consciousness through the transition between waking and sleep is the goal of many Eastern techniques, available to those skilled in yoga and meditation. The positive affirmation and visualization methods discussed in Chapter 10 also aim to maintain consciousness between waking and sleeping.

▶ **Positive affirmations.** See Chapter 10 for advice on working with positive affirmations. You may find that the positive affirmation makes it possible for you to become aware that you are dreaming, as you dream. As you fall asleep, try repeating: 'Tonight I, [name], will be consciously aware that I am dreaming.'

All these techniques can work, but that does not guarantee that a specific technique will work for you. If the first one you pick fails to yield results, try another. Or try combining techniques (e.g. magic question linked to trigger situation, plus either counting or positive affirmation). Allow yourself plenty of time to become aware that you are consciously dreaming – you are not in a race. Remember how long it takes children to learn to talk, and be prepared to give yourself as much time to become a lucid dreamer.

▶ 2 Learning how to exert your will in dreams

Far less has been written about how you can exert your will in a dream than on how to recognize that you are dreaming. Of course, during waking hours we do not normally reflect on how we exert our will, and perhaps we do not need to think about how we exert our will in dreams either. But in waking life performing some action does not normally put us in danger of falling asleep and, sometimes, exerting our will in dreams can wake us up.

One piece of advice is to act only as a casual observer of your dreams at first, or the lucid dream state might dissipate into wakefulness. Slowly insert volitional control. A simple way to begin to do this is to use the reality checks mentioned above.

If you suspect you are dreaming, you perform a reality check. You ask yourself whether your body can stretch until it is 50 feet high. It does so, and you know you are dreaming. This is a consciously willed body stretching, with the aim of determining whether you are dreaming. As you become more practised, you can begin to will more subtle events and actions, with ends and aims practically applicable in your waking life.

What are mutual dreams?

Mutual dreams are shared dreams – they occur when two or more people share a dream. In the Japanese folk tale with which we opened this chapter the servant Tarokaja and his lord experience a mutual dream.

In this book we shall consider only mutual dreams shared by two people whom we shall call dream partners. In waking life, dream partners need not be master and servant! They could be life partners, business partners, a parent and his or her child, two friends, etc. Like Tarokaja and his lord, they must trust each other implicitly and be motivated to work together to achieve shared goals. Unlike Tarokaja and his lord, who did not plan their mutual dream, dream partners who plan to have mutual dreams must each be willing to keep a dream journal, and to share the tiniest details of their dreams with each other.

Unlike lucid dreams, which have been investigated extensively in sleep research centres, mutual dreams have received little, if any, attention from the scientific community.

PLANNED MUTUAL DREAMS

The links between mutual dreaming and lucidity are not clear; however, it seems likely that:

▶ the experience of planned mutual dreams will be enhanced for both dream partners if they are both willing to try to achieve lucidity

▶ dream partners stand a far higher chance of bringing about a planned mutual dream if at least one of them is regularly aware that he or she dreams.

Planned mutual dreams need not necessarily involve the partners meeting in the dream; each could dream separately about a given situation or event. But many mutual dreamers aim to achieve dream meetings – where each dreams that he or she has met the other and they shared some dream experience or conversation.

The purposes of planned mutual dreaming are usually to enhance communication, increase levels of co-operation, collaboration and trust, and to lead to a fuller understanding between two people. It can also be used as an aid to conflict resolution.

ACHIEVING PLANNED, MUTUAL DREAMS

The main mechanism of achieving a planned mutual dream is to agree on a common intent with your partner. Perhaps you could agree to try to dream about overcoming a barrier to communication, or about solving financial problems, about how you both really feel about a prospective project, or whatever.

Once you have agreed on a potential topic, set a target night. On the target night, both partners should try to use one or other of the methods of dream incubation discussed in Chapter 10 – they need not use the same method. Positive affirmation can be particularly useful in increasing the likelihood of a mutual dream. If you aim to achieve a dream meeting, then just before falling asleep – whether this is in the same bed or geographically quite distant – you could each silently repeat: 'Tonight I, [name], will dream about and in co-operation with [partner's name]. If you want to share dream content, without meeting your partner, then repeat 'Tonight I, [name], will dream about [topic or project] in co-operation with [partner's name].'

The importance of dream recall and your dream journal cannot be overemphasized. In mutual dreaming, it is especially important to record your dream, in as much detail as you can, as soon as you wake. This way, you will be able to make accurate comparisons between your own and your partner's understanding and experience of the dream. You can also use your journals as a guide to whether or not you have achieved mutuality. When dream meetings occur, and you can both recall details of a shared experience, it is clear that you have achieved mutuality. But if you dream separately of a situation, it might take quite a bit of detective work to uncover the mutuality – you may each have dreamed symbolically, with little overlap between symbols, but much overlap between meanings. Comparing your and your partner's descriptions of a variety of dreams will give you insight into each other's symbolic thought, insight that you can bring to identifying mutual dreams.

UNPLANNED MUTUAL DREAMS

In a romantic context, unplanned mutual precognitive dreams are often reported. The scenario usually goes something like this: two people separately dream of meeting a specific stranger in a specific setting and a specific context. Later, the meeting occurs in waking life. One or other of the partners admits to dreaming of this meeting, and then so does the other. Often such dream meetings presage life-long, or highly significant, partnerships.

Case study: Sally and Tamara

The purposes of unplanned mutual dreams can sometimes be mysterious. Such a dream was experienced by Sally and Tamara. We met Tamara in Chapter 8: she has highly tuned psychic skills. She and Sally have been close friends since childhood and, as adults, shared an apartment. One morning Sally, a rabbit lover, announced she had dreamed about rabbits. Tamara, who is not fond of rabbits, expressed surprise as she too had dreamed about rabbits the night before. Both were amazed as it emerged that the details of their two dreams matched exactly, to the extent that Sally was able to say such and such happened (e.g. the little grey rabbit fell down a rabbit hole and disappeared) and Tamara was able to continue the story. Sally and Tamara were able to discuss their dream as if it were a book they had both read, or a film they had both seen. They found this experience highly entertaining, although any interpretation eluded them.

Food for thought: Further reading

Lucid Dreaming: The power of being awake and aware in your dreams (Ballantine Books, 1990) by Stephen LaBerge of Stanford University Sleep Research Centre, is a classic study in the field. LaBerge was responsible for developing the counting method for recognizing that you are in a dream. This book is fascinating and full of insights and information.

Mutual Dreaming: when two or more people share the same dream (Pocket Books, 1999) by Linda Lane Magallón is a comprehensive and authoritative guide to mutual dreaming.

Part two

The dreamer's dictionary

We are the music-makers,
And we are the dreamers of dreams,
Wandering by lone sea-breakers,
And sitting by desolate streams;
World-losers and world-forsakers,
On whom the pale moon gleams:
Yet we are the movers and shakers
Of the world for ever, it seems.

Arthur William Edgar O'Shaughnessy (1844–81), *Ode*

Notes on using this dictionary

We have already suggested that dream interpretation involves the ability to translate from the language of symbols into English (or any other natural language). This dictionary will help you in this task. But remember that the exact interpretation and significance of a dream symbol are specific to each individual – to you and you alone. So use this dictionary as a springboard for constructing your own interpretations. Use the records you make in your dream diary to start to build up your own dictionary of symbols, with meanings personal to you. Reread Chapter 2 if you need advice on starting a dream diary.

It is not possible to give potential meanings for every single symbol that could occur in your dreams. If a symbol appearing in your dreams is not listed here, look up something similar, or look at the group entries to get a general feel for what the symbol might mean.

GROUP ENTRIES

Group entries are given for common types of symbol – animals, flowers, fish, etc. In each case there are brief notes on the meaning of this whole class of symbol, then entries for a selection of things falling into the group. If your own dream symbol is not included, use something similar from the relevant group entry as a guide to drawing up your interpretation.

CONTRARIES AND INVERSIONS

An ancient doctrine, which was taken up by Freud, has it that dreams often speak to us in contraries – on immediate inspection it appears they are saying one thing, when, in fact, they are saying its opposite. For example, to dream of weeping, or being badly beaten, can symbolize both good luck and a change for the better. Similarly, to dream of a wedding can sometimes (not invariably) suggest a funeral, but to dream of a funeral, a coffin, a corpse, etc. can herald a wedding or other celebration. Or, again, to dream of finding money can sometimes mean its loss.

You will need to be alert to the possibility that your dreams are speaking in contraries when attempting to reach an interpretation.

A

abyss The bottomless chasm is traditionally a symbol of despair, or chaos, but it need not have these connotations for you, because the mechanism of contraries may be at work. If you manage to cross, or move around, an abyss, it can be a positive sign that you have the abilities to overcome obstacles. If you fall into an abyss, take it as a warning to be on your guard against obstacles that could prevent you from fulfilling some important aim.

acting *See* theatre.

adultery The meaning depends on the circumstances. Are you the adulterer? If so, examine the priorities in your life and determine whether some course of action currently important to you is in line with your true vision and values. Did you resist adultery? If so, your dream is telling you that you have the strength to resist a currently beguiling, but dangerous, temptation – not necessarily in a relationship. Were you the one being cheated on? If so, your dream could be telling you something about how others perceive you – as easily fooled and someone to be taken for granted. If you think this is possible, try to be more assertive and to make sure others are aware of your needs.

aeroplane/airport As discussed in Chapter 5, aeroplanes feature in many anxiety dreams. They could also symbolize isolation – sealed environments miles up in the alien sky. But, more positively, the plane can also be a powerful symbol of liberation, and almost boundless possibility – the modern version of the fairy-tale flying carpet. If you are the pilot, that could symbolize that you have the skill to bring off some important deal or discovery. Airports can be confusing places. A dream of an airport may indicate that you have to sit down and work through all the implications of a current problem, or it could indicate that you will soon be receiving something from distant lands – news, a gift or visitors.

ageing To dream of ageing can be a positive sign of continuing good health, or a more mixed sign that you are not taking basic steps to ensure that you remain in good health. Do you need to change your diet or quit smoking? Dreaming of ageing can also be about balance. It can indicate the need to acknowledge the importance of older people, or an older person, in your life and the need to give them more of your time and energy. Alternatively, if you care for an elderly relative, it could indicate that you need to give yourself more time.

airship A dream suggesting you should try to develop a wider perspective on some problem.

aisle What sort of aisle is it? A church aisle will mean something different from the aisle in a theatre or a cinema. The aisle may also mean different things to women and men. For a woman, a church aisle may symbolize a path she has to travel alone, to reach some important goal. For a man, it may just indicate one possible route through a difficult problem. Cinema and theatre aisles may indicate that, after a period of relative quiet, some new excitement is about to enter your life.

altar What sort of altar was it? An altar in a church? Or a simple stone on a barren hillside? What happened at the altar? A marriage? A sacrifice? You will need to consider questions such as this before decoding your dream, but, in general, altars are positive symbols indicating good fortune. If you dream of stumbling at an altar, that could be a symbol of the need to confront some guilt you currently refuse to acknowledge.

ambulance Generally considered an unlucky sign. To dream of an ambulance could indicate that someone you love is in danger. Conversely, if you know someone you love to be in danger, then to dream of an ambulance could indicate that they will soon be out of danger.

anchor Dreaming of an anchor can be a forewarning of danger, or a hint that you should take more care when undertaking ordinary activities, such as driving. An anchor, especially one being lowered, can indicate anxiety about the unknown, or fear of trying something new.

angels Angels usually symbolize protection – the protection of a friend, your partner, or some archetypal figure. Dreaming of an angel could prompt you to acknowledge the gifts this protecting presence brings to your life and prevent you from falling into taking him or her for granted. Or perhaps the dream could prod you to think about how you act to protect other people who are important in your life.

anger Was the anger directed at you? Or were you the one showing anger? Was the anger justified, or not? Your own justified anger could refer to some legitimate cause demanding your attention – perhaps a political cause. Your own irrational anger could be a way for your subconscious to force you to confront the ways in which you waste your emotional energy. If other people direct their anger at you, do a mental audit to see whether you have been behaving badly towards friends, family members or colleagues.

Animals

Animals can be classified in various ways, as wild animals, farm animals or pets, as mammals or reptiles, as four legged, or not, etc. Your own method of classification, together with your own personal experience of animals and the nature of the animal appearing in your dream will influence your interpretation. But, in general, animals can stand for the need to embrace our animal natures (i.e. the more physical aspects of our lives and personalities). Tamed animals, for example pets and farm animals, can symbolize our ability to, or our need to, tame more animalistic aspects of our personalities, such as aggression. Contrariwise, they may be warning us against passivity. Wild animals generally celebrate the power and strength of our animal natures. Creeping or crawling animals could symbolize our need to be braver in spiritual matters. Fast-moving animals, such as a cheetah, could symbolize rapid spiritual progress. Note that it is possible to give only cursory meanings here; much will depend on your personal circumstances and attitudes. **Cow:** you may soon be able to breathe more easily over some problem that has been bothering you. **Sheep:** expect to receive a surprise parcel.

Pig: illness or a successful journey, depending on the context. **Lion:** spiritual transformation and courage. **Tiger:** *see* the discussion in Louise's dream, Chapter 3. **Zebra:** beware deception by someone you trust. **Cat:** expect a visit from a stranger, or beware threats to your health, depending on the context; a cat washing itself may foretell a change of weather. **Dog:** this can be an unlucky symbol.

apparition A dream of an apparition could be asking you to think about divination, psychic powers and the role insight and intuition play in your life. If you do not regard yourself as particularly insightful, perhaps this dream is telling you that you have untapped powers that you could usefully deploy. If you frequently rely on intuition and inspiration, perhaps the dream is emphasizing your skills, or demanding that you think about how to expand them.

applause On the surface, this is a symbol of public recognition for a job well done. But the mechanism of contraries may be at work, so be on your guard against pride, arrogance, or taking the credit where credit is not really due. If you are applauding another, this could be a hint either that you are too lavish with insincere praise, or that you do not praise others enough for their efforts.

apples A generally positive symbol. Ripe apples can signify domestic happiness. Unripe apples can be a hint that you need to be more forgiving. A bowl of apples, especially older, wrinkled apples, can suggest that you will successfully circumvent potential hardship. Apples can sometimes represent irresistible temptation.

arch Is the arch complete or broken? What is it made of? Masonry, branches, or what? All these factors figure in the meaning of the symbol. Arches often symbolize paths. If the arch is complete, a path you are following will bear positive results. If it is broken, your route is possibly leading to a dead end. If the arch is of brick or stone, the path you are following could lead to some enduring result. If it is of branches, the result will be short lasting, although important.

armour A knight in shining armour can carry a meaning opposite to that of rescue – it can symbolize betrayal, but it all depends on context.

ashes Ashes are often interpreted as a symbol of good luck, especially of financial good luck. Sometimes ashes indicate a coming inheritance. If you dream of pictures in ashes, the pictures themselves have prophetic significance.

asteroid The dream could be emphasizing that you are at the mercy of forces you cannot control. To dream of an asteroid can indicate coming change, perhaps sudden, violent change, accompanied by shock, surprise or astonishment. Expect the unexpected.

attic For older people, attic dreams often symbolize domesticity and family life. An empty or dirty attic can indicate that you need to acknowledge unhappiness in some area of your home life. A clean but cluttered attic indicates fulfilment – but the nature of the fulfilment depends on the type of clutter. Toys can indicate your own childhood, or your children. Books can indicate the years you spent as a student, or any type of intellectual endeavour. Clothes can indicate the events for which they were worn. For younger people, attic dreams can symbolize the need to confront hidden fears.

aunt The aunt can represent an archetypal wise woman, a source of concerned but dispassionate help and advice. Perhaps this dream is indicating that you should relax enough to rely on such a figure more, or that you need to find such a figure for yourself, or even that you have the power to become such a figure to someone else. *See* Louise's dream, Chapter 3.

avalanche Were you caught in an avalanche? Or did you merely witness one? If you were a witness, were others buried, or not? To witness an avalanche, without casualties, can indicate tumultuous change in the world around you, which will affect you only indirectly. If there were casualties, you will need to be prepared to deal more closely with the fallout from change. If you were caught in the avalanche, take this as a warning. Great caution is required in the coming months.

avarice Are you the one showing meanness, or is meanness being shown to you? In either case, this might really be a dream about generosity, because the mechanism of contraries could be at work. If you dream of being avaricious, you probably show great generosity of spirit, perhaps unacknowledged by others. If you are the victim of avarice, perhaps you are the fortunate recipient of great, but as yet unacknowledged, generosity. The dream could be prompting you to acknowledge your good fortune.

B

baby Was the baby awake, or sleeping? Crying or laughing? Sitting or crawling? Was it your baby? Factors such as these have to be taken into account when decoding dreams of babies, also any other relevant factors, such as whether you are pregnant. But, in general, a baby is a symbol of hope and new opportunity. It indicates joy and a blessing that may, nevertheless, bring with it hard work and confusion.

baker To dream of a baker can indicate good health, especially for children.

ball A bouncing ball can indicate the timespan to some event – the number of bounces showing years, months, weeks or days. Playing ball games can indicate the competitive spirit. A ball, in the sense of a grand dance, has the same meaning as a party – *see that entry*.

balloon Was the balloon floating upwards, sinking or on a level? If it was floating, that could indicate good fortune, or good news, coming your way. If it was sinking, that could indicate bad luck or bad news. If it was on a level, things will continue much as they are. To dream of a child playing with a balloon is almost always favourable.

banquet What sort of banquet? Were you the host? How many guests? Were there any empty places at the table? You must consider questions such as these when trying to decipher your dream. In general, a lavish banquet, especially where you are the host, indicates abundance in your life, although, by the mechanism of contraries, it could indicate a time of belt tightening. Empty places at the table could indicate that strangers will soon be coming into your life, or that a family feud will soon be resolved. If the guests argue during the meal, that could indicate discord in some area of your life.

bath This can be a symbol of vulnerability. Are there areas of your life where you are vulnerable to surprise attack or ambush?

It can also be a symbol of the need for purification. Do you have unresolved guilt that you need to confront and overcome? A warm, scented bath can indicate sensual pleasures. A cold bath can indicate a denial of the pleasures of the body.

bed A bed may symbolize security; by way of contrast, a dream of a bed may be concerned, obliquely, with death, especially if the foot of the bed is towards the door. Interrupted bed making can be a warning of problems to come. The way in which occupants get out of the bed can be significant. If they get out backwards, or on the right, that can be a symbol of good luck; if on the left, that can be a symbol if ill luck, as can a dream of someone sitting on a bed.

beggar To dream of meeting a beggar can be a sign of good luck to come.

bereavement By the mechanism of contraries, a dream of bereavement may indicate joyous news to come, such as a marriage or a birth. Alternatively, a dream of bereavement may express justified anxiety about loss of any type. Sometimes, this may be a prophetic dream.

Birds

Remember that your own experience of, and attitudes towards, birds will greatly influence your interpretation, as will the specific nature of any species you see in your dream. Also think about the way in which you might classify the bird – as caged, predatory, songbird, flightless bird, etc. But, in general, birds can represent rationality, intellect, the mind and mental activities. Note that it is possible to give only cursory meanings here, and much will depend on the dream context and surrounding symbols. **Geese and eagles:** *see* discussion in Chapter 7. **Owl:** often this is an unlucky portent. **Peacock:** some wrong you have done has not gone unnoticed and you should expect to be made to pay. **Caged birds:** you need to give some new idea free rein and think through all the implications, but *see also* Louise's dream, Chapter 3. **Songbirds:** an intellectual pathway will lead you to an unexpected and wonderful destination. **Birds we eat:** chickens, ducks, turkeys, etc. often symbolize the need to be more rational in our approach to some issue. **Flightless birds:** these symbolize an emotion that needs to be curbed.

birth This symbol has different meanings for men and women. Among women, the meaning changes depending on whether she is of childbearing age or not, is pregnant or not, wishes to become pregnant or not, etc. You must examine the circumstances of your own life before trying to interpret this symbol, but it general it indicates happiness to come and new beginnings, not just literal births, for example a new beginning in your career or in relationships.

birthday The significance of a dream of your birthday depends on the timing and on your attitude in the dream. If you were miserable on your dream birthday, this could be a warning of troubles ahead. If you were happy, it could indicate good times ahead. If you received lots of presents, it indicates material gain, through chance, rather than hard work, for example by a win on the lottery. If you dream of your birthday when it is still months away, that is unlucky. If your dream occurs during the few days before your birthday, that is lucky. To dream of your birthday in the few days that follow it could be insignificant.

blood In a healthy person, to dream of drawing blood, or of bleeding, can indicate that you are soon to fulfil an outstanding obligation, or that you will have success in some new enterprise. In a sick person, to dream of blood can be an expression of anxiety about the disease.

boats To decipher this symbol, you need to think about the conditions of the boat in your dream. Was it in dry dock? If so, this can indicate bad luck to come. Was it bobbing merrily on calm waters? If so, you are entering a period of calm in your personal life. Was it tossed by huge waves? If so, expect difficulties ahead.

Body parts

Dreams of the human body vary greatly in meaning. Much depends on your age, sex, state of health and attitudes towards your own body. Often, dreams of the body are concerned with your bodily health; *see* Chapter 8. In other cases, the body can stand for opportunities and obstacles, possibilities and dead-ends in your path through life. Note that it is possible to give only cursory meanings here; much will depend on the specific details of your dream. **Head, face and hair:** these are all multi-layered symbols and it is difficult to generalize on meanings, but often hair can symbolize your sexuality, eyes your soul, and your face the mask you choose to present to the world. **Upper body and arms:** dreams of this region of your body can symbolize the need not to completely neglect the opportunities of the physical world around us in favour of less material pursuits. **Pelvic region:** this can symbolize sexuality and lust in a quite straightforward way, or passion, energy and fire as they manifest in all aspects of our lives. **Legs and feet:** often dreams of the legs and feet concern our need to become more centred or grounded, or the need to meditate on, or contemplate, our condition.

books If books appear in a dream, you can sometimes take this as an indication that you are neglecting to nourish your mind, and your subconscious is trying to prod you into taking up a new branch of learning or furthering an old skill.

bricks/building A dream of bricks, or one in which you are building, can indicate that you are troubled by unfulfilled desires – especially if the building is never completed, or if it topples the minute you have finished it. Alternatively, the activity of building can indicate that you are in danger of yielding to some dangerous temptation.

bride/bridegroom To dream of being or observing a bride or bridegroom is generally a positive omen, but, by the mechanism of contraries, unfortunate interpretations, such as of loss or bereavement, must be considered. The precise nature of the interpretation depends partly on your own circumstance – are you married or single or, if married, happily or not? – and partly on the circumstances of your dream. Was the bride/groom happy? What were the details of his or her clothes? If you were not yourself the bride or groom, did you touch him or her? If so, expect good news.

bridges The meaning of bridges is often straightforward; you have an opportunity to heal old wounds or patch up feuds.

broom To dream of a broom, or any type of brush for sweeping, is an indication that you require protection from, and should be on your guard against, menacing forces. Perhaps a friend or a family member is about to be swept away. If a broom handle breaks in your dream, that could indicate financial troubles ahead. A dream of a broom can also indicate that a stranger is about to enter your life – one whose intentions are not altogether good.

brother The meaning depends on your circumstances. Are you male or female? Do you get on well with your brother, or are you engaged in a feud? If you are engaged in a feud, the dream could be a hint that you should take the initiative, and try to patch things up. If relations with your brother are cordial, this dream can portend a period of great security in your life. *See also* sister.

bucket If a non-pregnant woman of childbearing age dreams of a bucket, this can be a sign that she will soon become pregnant. For others, it can be a sign that they will soon have a reason to throw a party. To dream of losing a bucket, or of an upturned bucket, can be a sign of coming bad luck.

bumble bee To dream of catching a bumblebee can be a symbol of luck, especially of financial gain. To dream of a bumblebee entering a house can be a warning of a coming death; alternatively, it can symbolize the coming of a stranger. If you drove a bumblebee out of a house in your dream, that can be a sign of coming ill luck.

burial By the mechanism of contraries, this indicates that you will probably be hearing good news in the coming days, or that sickness, especially diseases of the respiratory tract, or ill luck can be averted. A dream of a burial can also indicate that you are now able to tackle some long-term problem that has plagued you – for example you will now be able to control your wicked temper, or your drinking, or whatever.

burning If you are burned in a dream, this can indicate coming financial gain. If you witness a tree, bush or forest burning, this can indicate good luck. But if you witness a building burning, this can indicate that you should be on your guard against those who may not wish you well. You will almost certainly prevail against such people, if, in your dream, firemen extinguish the blaze.

butterflies To dream of a swarm of butterflies can indicate a coming death. A single butterfly can indicate a happiness to come. The colour of the dream butterfly is significant. If it is white, this is a lucky symbol and can indicate improving health, especially digestive health. If the butterfly is drab coloured, this is not a good sign and can indicate stomach problems.

C

cake What sort of a cake is it? Christmas, wedding, christening and birthday cakes have different significance, depending on your individual circumstances – although all are lucky. To dream of baking, buying or eating cake are all lucky dreams, indicating material gain and domestic happiness.

camera To dream of a camera can emphasize the need to tell, or discover, the truth in some important matter, even if the truth is painful.

candles If, in your dream, a single candle is left to burn until it goes out, that could indicate misery ahead. If the candle never burns down, that indicates coming happiness, or it can sometimes indicate that you will soon receive a welcome letter. Unlit candles signify protection. To dream of three candles, burning together, can indicate either a wedding or a death. To dream of lighting a candle can indicate coming financial hardship.

car What type of car? A luxury car, or something more humble? A stationary car, or one travelling at speed? All these things must be considered when interpreting this symbol; however, it is generally a sign that you are dissatisfied with some aspect of your life and need to take firm action in order to change direction.

cards, greeting You will soon receive significant documents or letters through the post.

cards, playing If you dream of winning a card game, that can indicate unhappiness in your marriage or relationship. If you lose at cards, that can indicate relationship happiness. If you dream predominantly of hearts or clubs, that can indicate strife; spades, especially the ace, can indicate a coming death, and diamonds infidelity.

cards, tarot If you regularly use the tarot cards, you may find symbols from the tarot incorporated in your dreams; if so, they generally have the same significance as you would give them in your waking life. If you are not familiar with the tarot, and find yourself dreaming of one of the cards, this may indicate that you do not allow the intuitive, inspirational side of yourself sufficient voice when making your decisions.

carols To dream of carols outside the festive season is a symbol of ill luck, as is dreaming of anything associated with Christmas outside the season. At Christmas, dreaming of carols is a neutral symbol: most likely carols occur in your dreams because you have heard them sung during the day. If you dream of turning carol singers from your door, that also indicates bad luck.

chair If you dream of sitting in a chair as soon as someone has vacated it, your own fate will closely mirror that of the other person. To dream of picking up a chair and turning it around means that your luck will soon change, for better or for worse. To dream of a chair placed firmly with its back to you means you will soon be involved in a lengthy quarrel.

child/children The interpretation of this symbol depends on your circumstances – do you have children, or not? Do you want children, or not? Are you male or female? By the mechanism of contraries, to dream of a child or children can often be a sign of trouble to come, either for yourself or for your family. However, such a dream could indicate the success of an enterprise, or a destination safely reached. The child can also be an archetypal symbol of joy, innocence and trust. *See also* Mary's dream, Chapter 5.

cigarettes If you smoke, to dream of cigarettes can be a way for your subconscious to prod you into quitting. Even your dreams are telling you to stop now! For both smokers and non-smokers, dreams of cigarettes can foreshadow respiratory illness. To dream of quitting, crushing cigarettes or stepping on cigarette packets are all lucky symbols.

circus If your dream features the ringmaster, this can be a hint that you need to be more concerned about the impression you are making on others. If it features the big top, you need to be concerned about maintaining a happy home environment. Accompanying children to the circus is generally a lucky portent; going alone can indicate coming hardship.

city Are you a city dweller, or not? Do you enjoy the energy of cities, or find yourself exhausted by it? Is the city you dreamed of a recognizable place, for example London or New York, or not? All these factors must be taken into account when analysing your dream but, in general, to dream of a city indicates confusion and obstacles to achieving your end. *See* Edward's dream, Chapter 4.

classroom If you are a teacher, you could dream of a classroom simply because that is where you spend most of your time. For other people, a classroom can indicate the need to confront some deep-rooted problem of long standing. *See* Mary's dream, Chapter 5.

cliffs Cliffs are a literal boundary between land and sea, and symbolize boundaries and changes of all sorts. To find the boundary referred to by your own dream, you will have to consider the circumstances of your own life.

Clothes

The precise interpretation of a dream concerning cloth or clothing will depend on the context, surrounding symbols and your personal circumstances – for example, it will mean something different to tailors, fashion designers, models, etc. than to those who tend to pay little attention to clothes. The specific nature of the clothes appearing in your dream, their condition, the cloth they are made of, etc., are all important. However, in general, clothes can often symbolize our social natures, roles in society, or the public face we choose to present to the world. Note that it is possible to give only cursory meanings here; much will depend on the specific details of your dream. **Clean or new clothes:** you need to work at presenting a more positive image to the world. **Old or dirty clothes:** others can see through any pretence you attempt to hide behind. **Men's clothes:** if you are man, you need to moderate typically male traits in social settings and become less laddish; if you are a woman, you need to stand up to men in social settings. **Women's clothes:** if you are a woman, do not rely on getting your own way through using your sexuality to manipulate others; if you are a man, beware of women attempting to manipulate you. **Children's clothes:** you are honest and open in your dealings with others and this is appreciated. *See also* Louise's dream, Chapter 3.

clocks To dream of a clock is generally unlucky and can carry a warning, perhaps even of a death. Particularly worrying are: a clock falling down, stopping or striking at an inappropriate time; speaking while a clock strikes; a clock striking the wrong time. If two clocks strike together, two people's fates are intimately connected.

clouds The shape of the clouds is a key indicator of their meaning, as is their type: thunder clouds mean something different from puffy white clouds in a blue sky. But, in general, clouds can symbolize the power and importance of daydreams and visions. Perhaps you are being prompted to act to bring about your daydreams.

coffin By the mechanism of contraries, this is often a lucky symbol, suggesting continuing or improved good health for you or someone you love. If you suffer from joint pain, to dream of a coffin can sometimes indicate that the pain is about to go away.

Colours

Colours can sometimes be used for emphasis, or to intensify a dream sequence – sometimes even giving, or enhancing, a nightmarish quality. The exact interpretation of colours in dreams depends on your own awareness of colour and its role in your waking life. Most of us rely on our own individually developed and applied colour associations, more or less consciously, and these will persist between your waking and your dreaming life. However, there are some constants, and, in interpreting colour in your dreams, you can bear in mind the following pointers. **Red:** a lucky colour, especially indicating happiness. **Yellow:** a lucky colour indicating wealth. **Green:** this conventionally means envy, but can also indicate that you need to pay fine attention to detail. **Blue:** this conventionally means sadness, but in dreams it can mean mystery; it can be prompting you to attack problems and puzzles you have long left unsolved. **Orange:** orange can indicate new beginnings and new chances. **Brown:** brown can mean safety and the comforts of home. **Violet:** can be a warning against violence. **Pink:** this can symbolize babies or young children. **White:** perhaps unexpectedly, white can indicate sadness, and mourning. **Black:** can symbolize power. In dreams, colour is often used to express emotions or moods. Drab, colourless dreams tend to accompany depression, or misery, and are a feature of dreams foretelling misery and anxiety dreams, etc. These rules of thumb do not apply if you are taking any sort of medication, or illegal drugs, drink excessive alcohol, or have an addiction to any substance, as any of these could produce vividly coloured dreams of little significance.

colleagues Often we dream of colleagues simply because we spend so much time with them. Often these are anxiety dreams with a work theme. Sometimes dreams can convey warnings that our colleagues are motivated by politics to undermine our own positions. If you get on well with your colleagues, negative dreams can be quite upsetting, but take their warnings seriously.

comet This dream symbol often foretells disaster or confusion.

commuting To dream of commuting can be a sign that you need to pay more attention to your mental health, especially your stress levels. Perhaps you should also consider having a physical check-up, paying particular attention to your blood pressure.

cooking A lucky symbol. For a woman who juggles work and family, it foretells both domestic happiness and career success.

corpse By the mechanism of contraries, this can be a lucky dream, foretelling a widening circle of friendships. It can also indicate continuing good, or improving, health. There is an old superstition that recommends touching the corpse if you do not wish to dream of the dead person.

counting *See* measuring.

cousin Like dreaming of other family members, the significance of a dream of your cousin depends largely on your relations with that person. Are relations good or bad? If bad, your subconscious is probably prodding you to take the initiative and try to patch up any quarrel; if good, the dream indicates the protective nature of your relationship.

crash Do not automatically take a dream of a crash, of any sort, as prophetic. It may be, but it may also be an expression of anxiety, or even a prod from your subconscious that you ought to take steps to ensure that you know what to do if ever confronted with a crash (i.e. take some first-aid classes).

crowds A crowd often symbolizes obstacles in your path on the road to fulfilling your ambitions. It can also indicate confusion and desire. *See* Louise's dream, Chapter 3.

crown By the law of contraries, to dream of a crown can indicate coming financial hardship, even the failing of a business venture, and the possible loss of a job. The richer and more splendid the crown, the worse the omen.

cutlery To dream of a fork can mean a woman will be visiting you soon; a knife indicates a man, and a spoon a baby or child.

D

. . . .

dancing Who was dancing? And why? You need to think over these questions before trying to interpret your dream but, in general, dreams of dancing are very favourable, indicating great social success, and sometimes having sexual connotations.

danger By the mechanism of contraries, this usually indicates that some danger, physical, emotional or spiritual, is behind you, enabling you to move on and see that what is past is over and gone.

daughter *See* child/children.

dawn A happy symbol, signifying new beginnings, hope and opportunity.

dead According to the Hippocratic treatise *On Regimen*, dreams of the dead stand for the food one has eaten 'for from the dead come nourishment and growth and seed'. To dream of someone now dead is nearly always significant, but the particular significance for you will depend on your relationship to the dead person.

death/dying By the mechanism of contraries, this is usually a dream with a positive message. You will soon be freed from worries, or hear good news.

demolition Take courage – you can demolish obstacles in your path, even if this now seems impossible, and will eventually be able to place something newer and better where once there was a derelict place in your mind or heart.

dentist To dream of dentists is usually a straightforward expression of fear – unless you are a dentist yourself, or closely related to one, in which case the symbol may not be significant. A dream of a dentist can also indicate vanity. *See also* teeth.

desert The desert often symbolizes freedom or spiritual enlightenment. Your subconscious is prodding you to pay attention to your spirit – perhaps you should investigate new methods of self-understanding such as meditation.

devil By the mechanism of contraries, this could be a dream of good fortune. However, it might be a sign that you should re-examine some old guilt or secret, and attempt to make recompense for old wrongs. If you were fighting with the devil, you should perhaps get ready for some fierce battles with more mundane opponents over some cause in which you passionately believe.

diary If you dream of keeping your dream diary, this is most likely a neutral result of thinking about it during the day. If you dream of old diaries, what was the context? Could this be a divinatory dream about the past? Have you any way of checking information you receive via dream diaries – yours or other people's?

dice This could be a dream warning you to evaluate your current actions to check that they are genuinely in line with your vision and values. A spectacular win at dice could, by the law of contraries, presage a spectacular financial loss, perhaps on the stock market.

dirt A lucky symbol. Excessive cleaning can be a sign of ill luck – you are cleaning your luck away. This could mean alienating a friend, for example.

disaster What is the nature of the disaster? And what type of dream is this? Warning or anxiety? You will need to answer questions such as these before interpreting a dream of disaster, but remember that by the mechanism of contraries, this could, in fact, be a dream of extreme good luck.

disease The meaning will vary according to your health and circumstances but, in general, it is wise to take dreams of sickness and disease seriously, and to take them as warnings. Do you have any symptoms you are trying to ignore? If so, consult a doctor and get a check-up. *See also* illness.

diving A dream of diving can indicate confidence in your own skills and abilities, or your sense of alienation, perhaps at your workplace. This can be a dream warning of unexpected danger.

divorce The precise meaning of this dream depends on your circumstances. But for married people or those about to wed, by the law of contraries, it can indicate a long and happy marriage. For those who have no plans to marry, it can be an oblique way of referring to other types of rupture, in friendships, in your career, etc.

doctor If you are a doctor, or have seen a doctor on the day before your dream, this dream figure could be a result of your daytime experience. For others, a doctor generally symbolizes either a warning not to ignore worrying symptoms, or the need to take positive steps to improve your health, for example by changing your diet. Sometimes a doctor can symbolize improvement in your health.

dolphin To dream of a dolphin may be a sign of impending travel, usually a holiday rather than a business trip or a house move. It may also be a sign that you are capable of solving deep-seated problems through your own efforts. *See also* animals *and* fish.

dreams/dreaming Dreaming of dreams and dreaming can be very confusing, and can prompt doubts about the nature of reality when you wake up. Dreams of dreaming are usually an invitation to explore metaphysical and philosophical questions, or a hint that you are not stretching and challenging your mental powers to their full capacity.

drinking If you dream of someone spilling drink, especially beer or wine, that can be considered a lucky portent. If you dream of two people sharing a cup, that can indicate trouble ahead, perhaps sickness.

driving What was the condition of the car and what were the road conditions? In general, dreams of driving signify travel, especially business travel, and financial good fortune.

dwarves Often dreams of dwarves concern friendship. Your subconscious may be telling you not to take a friend for granted, or to make excessive and prolonged demands without giving anything in return. Or a dwarf could be warning you against the motives of a false friend. The context of the dream may suggest ways in which you can be of help or service to your friends.

E

. . . .

ears If you dream of ringing in your ears, this can be a sign that you have as yet unacknowledged psychic abilities, which you should henceforward exploit. Alternatively, it can mean that you are about to hear some bad news. If you dream of your ear or your cheek tingling, beware of someone trying to undermine your reputation.

Earth, the According to the Hippocratic treatise *On Regimen*, the Earth stands for the dreamer's flesh. To dream of the Earth can be a sign that you need to pay close attention to ways to nourish yourself or those around you. Or it could be a dream expressive of environmental anxiety.

earthquake According to the Hippocratic treatise *On Regimen*, an earthquake stands for physiological change. If you dream of an earthquake, expect the unexpected in all spheres of your life.

eating What were you eating? And under what circumstances? To eat alone can be a symbol of alienation and unhappiness with your social life. To eat with friends can symbolize that your social world is about to expand in exciting ways. Overeating can be an obvious symbol of the need for restraint.

echo If you dream of an echo, expect events, actions or people from your past to make a sudden reappearance in your life. Perhaps you need to confront some old guilt, or mend a long-broken relationship.

eclipse, lunar If you dream of a lunar eclipse, this could be a message from your subconscious that you are neglecting the more intuitive and emotional aspects of your personality. You should open up to the feminine, even if you are male – all aspects of your personality should be in balance for a happy mental life.

eclipse, solar If you dream of a solar eclipse, this could be a message from your subconscious that you do not pay enough attention to the demands of reason and the intellect in your life, but depend too much on intuition. Open up to masculine energies, even if you are female – all aspects of your personality need to be in balance for a happy mental life.

education If you are a teacher, or currently a student, this dream will mean different things for you than for others, and may be a neutral symbol, reflecting your day-to-day experiences. For others, it could be a prod from your subconscious that you would benefit from undertaking a course of study, or, especially, training linked to your professional life. Investigate whether your employer would fund such training for you.

eggs Did you dream of one egg, or a clutch of eggs? A single egg can be unlucky, a clutch can represent prosperity. If you are sick, dreaming of eggs can symbolize a return to health. To dream of a double-yolked egg can foretell a wedding. Breaking eggs generally signifies trouble ahead. If you dream of crushing eggshells, that indicates you have the inner resources to deal with psychic forces opposing you.

electricity To dream of electrical wires, electrical goods, electrical shocks, etc. indicates that you have to contend with powers beyond your control. You will be able to control these powers through your own ingenuity, but will not prevail without first undergoing some pain and difficulty.

elf A dream of friendship. *See also* dwarves.

emptiness A dream of emptiness – empty space, empty rooms, empty vessels, empty pockets, and so on – can indicate that you are time famished, and need to simplify your life, manage your time better, and make more time for yourself and your loved ones.

endings A dream of an ending, to a relationship, a job or a simple task, can indicate new beginnings.

engaged couple/engagement ring If you are unmarried, to dream of topics connected with engagement can, by the mechanism of contraries, be a warning of relationship difficulties ahead. If you are married, to dream of engagement can reflect current problems in your relationship. Alternatively, for anybody, a dream of engagement can reflect a desire for security – think about how you could procure greater security for yourself in your waking life. To dream specifically of an engagement ring suggests you will soon need to show charity to your partner or, if single, to your most intimate friends.

engine To dream of engines, of any sort, can be a warning against overly extending yourself in debt, or of financial hardship to come. If you are a mechanic by trade, it can be a neutral symbol, reflecting your day-to-day activities.

envelopes These represent travel, especially business travel. They can also be a sign that you will soon receive important news. If you have difficulty opening an envelope in your dream, this can be a symbolic representation of obstacles in your path on the way to achieving a goal.

evening A dream set in the evening can foretell a loss of a treasured possession, perhaps an heirloom.

examination To dream of a physical examination, for example by a doctor, can be a warning to take some worrying symptoms seriously. To dream of a written or oral examination can be a sign that you are now ready to tackle a long-delayed, but important, task, with potential benefit to your personal life or career.

excrement By the mechanism of contraries, this can be a lucky symbol – especially dreams of stepping in (animal) excrement. If you dream that bird droppings fall on your clothes, that can foretell a very happy year ahead. If a woman of childbearing age dreams of a baby's dirty nappy, that can mean that she will soon become pregnant. In the sick, dreams of excrement can indicate a return to health. For everybody, such dreams indicate that powerful forces are working for our protection.

exercise This is often a straightforward message from your subconscious about your need for a balanced approach to exercise. You may need to take up exercise, do more exercise, or, if you already have a heavy exercise regime, to cut back. It can also be a symbolic representation of your financial status – if you found the exercise easy, you are in good financial health; if it was difficult, you need to budget more carefully.

exhaustion By the mechanism of contraries, this can mean that you will have all the energy you will need to face and overcome difficulties. Alternatively, it can be a straightforward warning that you need to rest and give in gracefully to the needs of your body.

explosion To dream of an explosion can indicate confusion on your part concerning some important issue, or that you have got some aspect of your life out of proportion and need to re-examine your vision and values. An explosion can also have sexual connotations, especially if you have recently entered a new relationship. It can also be a warning against imprudent waste of money. *See* Louise's dream, Chapter 3.

F

. . . .

face *See* body parts.

factory A dream of a factory can indicate dissatisfaction in your career, or suggest that you are needlessly suppressing your own creative urges because of undue concern about the reactions of others. The dream is telling you to think about the role of freedom in your own life – the more automated the factory, the more pressing your need.

fairy A dream of friendship. *See also* dwarves.

falling A dream about your relationship to those around you. This can represent your fear of failure and the worry that you are not living up to others' expectations. Contrariwise, it can represent liberation from social convention and the norms of the majority. Only you can decide which of these interpretations suits your current circumstances.

farm If you dream of a farm, expect a period of hard work ahead. If the farm looked prosperous, your hard work will be rewarded; if it looked neglected, your hard work will be in vain.

father Only you can interpret a dream of your father, since its significance depends on the details of your relationship. However, a dream of your father can sometimes indicate that you are struggling to find direction in your life and feel a childish need for authority, and someone to tell you what to do. The dream could be telling you that only you can sort out your problems; relying on others will get you nowhere. *See also* mother.

feather To dream of a black feather is unlucky, as is to dream of walking past a feather. However, if you dream of seeing a feather on the ground, and then picking it up, this represents a change in your luck and good times ahead.

fire If you dream of a fire blazing brightly, that indicates that a stranger is about to enter your life who will significantly increase your social circle. If the fire burns badly, that indicates family quarrels and dissension to come. A very smoky fire can indicate marital strife. A fire burning in a lopsided way can indicate a parting – perhaps foretelling a house move. If there are lots of sparks, you will soon be receiving important news. If the fire spits and roars, expect trouble from your boss. If you dream of someone poking at a fire, beware the questionable motives of false friends, especially at work. If you dream of building a fire, that can be a lucky sign; if you dream of a fire going out, that can be unlucky.

fireman This can mean that your family is about to be engulfed in a major quarrel or disagreement, but that together you have the resources necessary to put your problems behind you and move on with a united front.

Fish

Fish is used loosely here to include many forms of aquatic life – whales, sharks, crustaceans, etc. and also amphibians. Each type, and each member of each type, has its own particular associations and meanings, so giving general guidelines is difficult. Your own relationship with and attitudes to these creatures is the most important factor to consider in reaching an interpretation. You also need to consider surrounding symbols and the context and details of your dream. However, dreams of water-dwelling creatures often concern origins and beginnings – of ideas, people, lives, causes, etc. Note that it is possible to give only cursory meanings here; much will depend on specific details of your dream. **Octopus:** you find it difficult to leave the past behind and move on. **Starfish:** a new venture will have spectacular results in the short term, but will ultimately lead to disappointment. **Frogs:** the power of transformation is active in your life and will help you progress beyond an unpromising start. **Shellfish:** beware the destructive power of secrecy. **Fish with scales:** be alert to destructive repeating patterns in your life. **Whales:** you are supported by firm beginnings that give you the inner strength to face all challenges. *See also* dolphin *and* shark.

fireplace/fire accessories A dream of a fireplace can indicate new beginnings in your life. To dream of fire accessories (the poker, fire tongs, etc.) can indicate tears ahead. A dream of fire tongs can be a warning not to undertake a planned expedition the following day.

fishing If you are not an angler, to dream of fishing portends financial gain or a significant gift. If you dream of giving away fish, this can indicate a financial loss. If you are an angler, this may just be a neutral symbol, reflecting your day-to-day experience.

flags To dream of country flags, your own or that of another country, is usually a dream of some political significance. Is your subconscious prompting you to get involved with some international charity or an important social cause? To dream of bunting and festive flags generally indicates a carefree time ahead.

floating To dream of floating can indicate that you need a period of readjustment in your life – a time of quiet contemplation allowing you to take stock of your achievements and to prioritize your real needs and desires.

flood A huge deluge can symbolize uncontrolled and uncontrollable emotions, linked to someone to whom you feel attracted. Beware that he or she is not abusing your passion. A more gentle flood can indicate that you need to identify, and remove, obstacles blocking your path to a goal.

Flowers

The role that flowers play in your waking life is highly significant – for example, a florist or horticulturist will find meanings in flower dreams different from those of other people; indeed, for these people these dreams may sometimes be insignificant reflections of their daily activities. You also need to consider the context of the dream, surrounding symbols and the colour and condition of any flowers you dreamed of – for example, are they growing, dried or cut? Plants commonly considered weeds can also be significant. In general, flowers in dreams symbolize neglected or hidden talents, abilities or potentialities. Two types of flower dream have specific meanings. Red and white flowers mixed together in a dream can symbolize coming illness or ill luck. Dreams of taking flowers home from hospital are a bad omen, suggesting the dreamer will soon be visiting a hospital. Note that it is possible to give only cursory meanings here; much will depend on specific details of your dream. **Dried flowers:** you are letting a loving and nurturing instinct go to waste. Try to find a channel for all you have to give. **So-called weeds:** in all the bustle of your daily living, you are neglecting your most deeply held aims and ambitions. **Spring flowers and blossom:** your talents will soon find new outlets. Some flowers have traditional symbolic associations that may have meaning for you – for example, the rose can stand for perfection, the lily for purity.

flying To dream of flying through the air unaided indicates the degree of reality in your ambitions. If you achieve this feat easily, you will reach your ambitions; if you struggle to maintain height you are probably overreaching yourself and should try to be content with what you have. This can also be a dream suggesting you would benefit from taking a wider perspective on some problem. To dream of flying on a magic carpet suggests you would benefit from trying to recapture a sense of childlike wonder and delight in the world. *See also* aeroplane/airport and birds.

Food

What was the nature of the food and what was its condition? Where did you eat it, and why? Was it plentiful or rationed? Factors such as these are all-important, as are your waking attitudes to food – for example, if a vegetarian dreams of eating meat, this is a dream pregnant with meaning, whereas for a meat eater to dream of meat may be insignificant. In general, food and eating can symbolize your family life or your social life. A plentiful feast consumed in happy surroundings indicates a happy family life and a varied social life. A rationed meal in grim surroundings can indicate that you lack love and friendship in your life. Dreams of food can carry coded messages about the state of your body. Burned food, burned toast, burned meat, etc., can indicate health problems relating to the digestive system. Fruit and vegetables that have gone rotten can sometimes indicate unsuspected allergies or food intolerances. Dairy produce can indicate that you really do need to take care to eat a healthy diet. Sweet food such as puddings could, unsurprisingly, carry a clear warning that you should book a visit to the dentist. Bread, rice and potatoes can all indicate that you have taken a weight loss diet to extremes, and that you need to get your food intake back in balance – your body is telling you that its health is more important than a fashionable slimness.

fog A fairly straightforward symbol of secrecy and confusion. Are you trying to mislead another? If so, the dream is warning you not to become lost in your own deceptions. Sometimes fog can be a symbol of protection and the protective, not destructive, nature of secrecy.

forest If you are stressed, this is an excellent dream as it can mean you will soon achieve peace of mind and a calming of your shredded nerves.

friends The exact meaning will depend on the context of your dream and on your relationship with the friends involved. Often, dreams of friends concern ways in which we can help them through a difficult time. Or they may alert you for the first time that one of your friends is unhappy or in difficulty. Could you offer a sympathetic ear or practical help?

fruit Often, ripe fruit stands for reward – the rewards of hard work, effort, discipline or mental effort. Ripe fruit is an especially lucky symbol if you are about to take an exam. Unripe fruit suggests that you have started a project that you will not finish. Individual fruits have individual meanings, but these depend in large part on your attitude to the fruit – if you loathe bananas, bananas will mean something different for you than for a banana lover! A fruit bowl can symbolize generosity. Rotting fruit can symbolize neglect of domestic affairs.

G

gambling Gambling is, of course, about taking chances, and this is a dream about the role of chance in your life. But its exact interpretation will depend on whether your dream activity resulted in a win, or a loss, and on your waking attitude to risk. If you are risk averse, a gambling dream could be prompting you to open up to spontaneity; if you love risk, your dream could be warning you not to become foolhardy. By the mechanism of contraries, a dream of a big win may be a warning against loss, and a dream of loss may herald a gain of some sort. As discussed in Chapter 8, some dreams of gambling are prophetic and can be used to help you place bets.

garden/gardening If you are a keen gardener, this may be a neutral symbol. For others, this may be a dream about nurturing and building for the future. A neglected garden hints at neglect in your emotional life, with emphasis on the family. A beautiful, well-cared-for garden hints at domestic pleasures, security and long-term joy. A dream of a garden may also be about the role of artistic fulfilment in your life. Do you secretly hanker to take up painting or writing? If so, this dream could be telling you to give an artistic pursuit a try. Alternatively, gardens can stand for your need for privacy, or even for the role of secrecy in your life.

garlic This is often a dream about protection and cure, although for keen cooks it may be a neutral symbol drawing on their everyday activity. To dream of a clove of garlic can indicate either that you have the inner resources to deal with problems confronting you, or that some physical danger will be averted or overcome.

gate Gates allow us to pass through from one realm to another. This can be a dream of crossing thresholds to something exciting and desirable. An open gate can indicate that you will achieve your heart's desire, a closed gate that you will eventually attain your end only after surmounting various obstacles. A locked gate hints that you are most unlikely to attain your desires.

Geographical dreams

Geographical dreams are a loose category that includes all dreams with a setting that is quite real, but which is foreign to you – Australia, say, or China. Geographical dreams include dreams of globes, dreams of compasses, dreams of maps. There is a crossover with dreams of journeys. Dreams of individual countries may not be significant – if you are planning a holiday to that destination, for example, and have been reading tourist brochures. If dreams are significant, you must first decipher their importance by considering why you dreamed of that country. Do you want to go there? If so, was your dream wish fulfilment? Do you know someone from that country? In general, dreams of the north – frozen wastes, sweeping winds – can mean shamanism or white witchcraft, and they can be an indication that you should be open to white magic. Dreams of the south – hot sun, lapping sea, gentle breezes – can be a happy omen that your sex life is about to improve. Dreams of the east – any dream with an oriental setting – can indicate either that you need to show more respect to your elders, especially your parents, or that you need to take more care with your finances. Dreams of the American Wild West symbolize dissatisfaction with your life, and the desire to try something bold and new.

germs (bacteria, mould, etc.) This could be a warning that you are putting yourself in danger of physical illness by disregarding simple rules of hygiene, or a dream of less immediately obvious threats to your wellbeing, such as mental, emotional or spiritual health problems. Try some literal and metaphorical spring-cleaning.

giant A dream of friendship, warning you against making overly quick or glib judgements about others. The dream could be telling you to enjoy and celebrate the differences between people and to be more adventurous in your social life.

glass Glass can be an unlucky symbol in a dream, often presaging some unwelcome event. To see glass breaking can be a warning against travel of all kinds, but especially travel at sea, or it can be a warning about giving a false promise or oath, or about being aware that others may make false promises to you or swear a false oath against you.

globe The desire for adventure. *See also* geographical dreams.

gloves If you dream of dropping a glove and picking it up yourself, you will have a disappointment. If, however, someone else picks it up, you will have a pleasant surprise. If you dream of exchanging a pair of gloves with someone else – either as a gift or a loan – that can indicate a quarrel and a broken friendship or relationship.

gnome *See* dwarves.

goblet A goblet can indicate an open mind and receptivity to new ideas – attitudes that your dream is encouraging you to cultivate. This applies whatever the goblet is made of, and whatever its condition. However, both these factors influence the interpretation of your dream. An expensive goblet can warn against the charms of sloppy thinking; a simple goblet can be telling you not to overlook obvious truths.

goblin *See* dwarves.

gold *See* metals.

gossip Are you the gossip, or the subject of gossip? If you are the gossip, this could be a dream warning you to be more careful with the confidences of your friends. If you are being gossiped about, you are likely to receive some important news in the not-too-distant future. If you witness others gossiping about someone other than yourself, expect soon to be embroiled in a quarrel.

grandfather The grandfather figure can be a representation of the archetypal old wise man, representing an inner guiding wisdom, especially the wisdom inherent in older ideas and attitudes that you may otherwise be liable to dismiss as outdated.

grandmother The grandmother can be a representation of the archetypal old wise woman representing nurture, protection, intuition and creativity. Be open to these aspects of yourself and to older ideas or attitudes that you may otherwise be liable to dismiss.

grass Is this a well-tended lawn, or a field of rough grass? Is it green or parched? Factors such as these will influence your interpretation but, in general, grass can be a symbol of the power of mysterious forces in our lives, either psychic forces or the forces of nature.

grave By the mechanism of contraries, this need not be a grim dream. Often, a grave will represent healing, especially healing of reproductive, digestive or skin disorders. If you dream of meeting or parting at a grave, expect relationship difficulties ahead. If you dream of walking over a grave, that can be an unlucky portent.

greenhouse If you are a keen gardener, this may be a neutral symbol, reflecting your day-to-day experiences. For others, it may be a way to prod your conscious mind into re-examining childhood memories, in an effort to make sense of some aspect of your current life.

guns Were you loading the gun, or firing it? Or were you shot at, or a witness to a shooting? Whatever the specifics, dreams of guns can be warnings against giving way to strong feelings, or passions in inappropriate contexts. Guard against violence. Sometimes guns can be concerned with justice, or, more particularly, injustice.

H

. . . .

hair Hair can have various meanings. It can be a warning against, or prophetic of, travel, especially international travel. A dream of loss of hair can refer to some other sort of loss, perhaps financial or emotional. A dream of a woman with long hair can reflect relationship anxiety. By way of contrast, hair can represent fidelity in a relationship and protection from various ills, both physical and psychic. If, in your dream, you alter your hairstyle, expect to adopt some radical new approach to some problem in your waking life.

hairpins If you dream of a hairpin falling out, this probably means that someone desperately wants to talk to you or, at the very least, is thinking about you.

handkerchief To dream of a clean, freshly ironed handkerchief can be an unlucky sign. A handkerchief can mean tears.

hands *See* Body parts.

hat To dream of a hat can often be a reflection of anxiety about your social standing, or about how others perceive you, or it can contain messages about how you can manipulate others' perceptions of you. The dream is telling you to reflect on your various roles in life. *See also* the discussion of Freud on hats in Chapter 7.

head *See* Body parts.

headache/hangover This can be a simple warning against overindulgence in food or alcohol, or may have a message about your general state of health. Do not ignore worrying symptoms.

hearse By the mechanism of contraries, this may be a dream foretelling good news, such as financial gain or a promotion. However, if you dream of a hearse breaking off its journey, for whatever reason, expect bad news or a shock.

heat/being hot A dream of being hot, or of heat spreading over your body, can indicate that your life is about to change.

heroes/heroic acts Dreams of heroes and heroic acts can indicate determination – not giving in and not giving up. They can mean the determination to overcome adversity, or the determination that life should return to normal after a period of adversity.

hobby If you dream of your hobby, this is probably just a neutral symbol reflecting your day-to-day activities. If your hobby carries inherent dangers (e.g. extreme sports), the dream could be warning you to take the risks seriously and avoid becoming rash or overconfident. To dream of taking up a new hobby can be a prompt that you need to listen to others and accept compromise. To dream of leaving a hobby-related project unfinished can suggest you will still receive censure.

home If you dream of your childhood home, this can be a prompt that you need to re-examine childhood memories or confront long-standing guilt, or it can carry the message that the past is dead and gone and you are free to move on. To dream of your current home can be a neutral reflection of your daily experiences, or can be an indication that you can expect domestic satisfaction and harmony. If you now live in a country other than that in which you were born, to dream of home can carry political overtones that you should attempt to untangle.

honeymoon Are you married or not? Did you dream of your own or another's honeymoon? Such factors will influence your interpretation. In relationships of long standing, a dream of a honeymoon can signal the need to continue to work to together to keep the relationship fresh.

horse rider To dream of a horseman or woman is a lucky sign. Expect good news.

hospital If you work in a hospital, this dream may have neutral meaning for you, merely reflecting your daily experiences. For others, the meaning of the dream will depend in large part on whether you were a patient or a visitor to the hospital. If you were a patient, you are probably struggling unnecessarily with what seems like an insurmountable problem. If you could bring yourself to ask for help, you would probably find it resolved itself quite easily – you have become so entangled in your concern that you cannot see the wood for trees. If you dream of visiting a hospital, by the mechanism of contraries expect good news about a friend or relative.

host/hostess If you dream of presenting a gift to a host or hostess, that is a lucky sign. If you dreamed of being a generous host, expect new openings in your social life. If you dreamed of being a reluctant hostess, perhaps some of your acquaintances do not have your best interests at heart.

hotel This can symbolize irresponsibility and can be a warning that you should be more responsible, perhaps in your relationships, or that you should try to drop some of your responsibilities and have some fun – the meaning depends both on the context and your circumstances.

houses To dream of building a new house can foretell an injury. To dream of moving into a new house can foretell a pregnancy. Dreams of demolishing old houses can be about the importance of putting the past behind you, or about the need to avoid profligacy and waste. Dreams about selling houses can be about the need to shed overly demanding responsibilities – perhaps at work. *See also* India's dreams in Chapter 2 *and* Louise's dreams in Chapter 3.

housework If you are a woman, is your dream telling you that your family is treating you like a drudge? Go on strike! If you are a man, is your dream telling you that you should be helping out around the home more often?

hurricane This is a dream about overwhelming forces that will shape your life but which you are powerless to control, for example economic forces that cause your workplace to close. Prepare for difficulties ahead and try to keep your head below the parapet.

husband For a woman to dream of her husband often means she needs to think about the power and importance of the masculine in her life. Contrariwise, this can be a neutral symbol reflecting a woman's daily experiences, or can have a meaning that is entirely personal, depending solely on the couple's relationship and circumstances.

I

....

ice To dream of an icy landscape often carries the meaning that you need to spend some quiet time just thinking about your life as it is and reappraising your visions and values. After this period of stasis is over, you will be in a better position to meet challenges and forge ahead with plans and ambitions. Slipping on ice can be a symbolic representation of obstacles in your path to a goal.

ice skating This is a dream about co-operation on some major project, probably with a business, financial or political twist. It can hint at your need for co-operation from others, or at the importance of developing your own skills as a team player. Resist the urge to become a dominant leader.

Illness

Were you sick, or was another person the victim of disease? If the disease features you falling ill, take this as a general warning about your health, and take any preventive measures necessary. If you dream of others falling ill, be careful of other people's feelings for a while, as the dream could indicate a friendship under stress. Some specific diseases carry fairly specific meanings, although, as always, the exact interpretation will depend on you, and on your circumstances. Skin diseases, rashes of all sorts, can hint that you must take steps to stop other people undermining you, especially at work. Eye diseases can indicate that you need to do some hard thinking about a relationship. Dreams of your hair falling out can indicate that you are in a run-down state, and should consider a new health regime. Digestive diseases can indicate a generalized anxiety, which you need to resolve. Dreaming of breathing difficulty can indicate that you feel trapped, at work, at home, or in a problematic relationship, and that it is time to take some action. *See also* disease.

iceberg Usually a reasonably obvious symbol of powerful obstacles in your path – the danger is greater than you realize, but, with luck and skill, you will be able to find a way to fulfil your ambition.

icicles These can signal hidden dangers from unexpected quarters.

idleness By the mechanism of contraries, a dream of idleness can often herald a period of extremely hard work.

image To dream of your own image – in a photo, painting, wax doll, or whatever, can often signal that you are in danger from some unexpected quarter. Be extremely cautious in all your dealings. To dream of the image of another person, known to you, can indicate that you have ill feelings for this person, even if you do not acknowledge them at a conscious level. To dream of the image of someone unknown to you can indicate that a stranger is about to enter your life, to ill effect.

impotence For a man, this can be an anxiety dream or a health warning. For women, to dream of an impotent man can reflect either an ambivalent attitude to sex in general or to a particular sexual relationship. It can also express a great, but as yet unfulfilled, capacity to love.

incoherence If, in your dream, your speech becomes incoherent, this indicates the speedy resolution of deep confusion on some important matter. If you find others incoherent, a period of discord is likely to follow, especially in a business-related setting.

Insects

The meaning of a dream featuring insects will depend on your attitude to insects, and on your experience of them. It will also depend, to a large part, on which insect, or insects, are depicted and on surrounding symbols. But often such dreams concern disruptions to everyday life, ranging from trivial annoyances to major disasters. Insects can also symbolize the pangs of conscience, biting or stinging away at us. More positively, but rarely, insects can symbolize transcendence and transformative spiritual power (e.g. this could be the meaning of a caterpillar or of a scarab beetle). Note that it is possible to give only cursory meanings here; much will depend on specific details of your dream. **Stinging insects:** any feelings of self-reproach you currently experience are probably justified. **Biting insects:** disease or financial hardship are about to become important to you. **Ants:** symbolize hard work and a positive team spirit, or, alternatively, social repression. **Spiders:** can symbolize rivalry for power, particularly economic power, within a relationship. **Cockroaches:** symbolize problems with your housing – this could range from a leaking roof to being evicted at short notice. *See also* bumblebee *and* butterflies.

infection *See* Illness.

inferiority By the mechanism of contraries, to feel socially inferior in your dreams suggests a rapid improvement in your social circumstances, and a widening circle of friends. If, in your dreams, you feel that others are inferior to you, beware of arrogance in your dealings with others.

infidelity This may be a warning, perhaps your first, that all is not well in your relationship. That said, by the mechanism of contraries, it can indicate loyalty and mutual respect within a happy relationship.

ink To dream of spilling ink is often an unlucky portent.

insomnia To dream of insomnia signals a need to set priorities in your life and to get to grips with time management.

instruments, musical If you are a musician, your interpretation will be different from that of non-musicians; the dream may even be insignificant for you. For others, instruments symbolize the need for harmony between different aspects of the personality, so check that some aspect of your life has not become unbalanced, or that a trivial issue has not gained disproportionate importance. In addition, stringed instruments can symbolize the need to pay attention to detail, wind instruments the need to think before you speak, brass instruments the dangers of boasting, and percussion instruments the necessity of standing up for yourself in an argument.

instruments, surgical Surgical instruments often symbolize the need for precision and careful preparation when attempting to put a plan into practice. For surgeons, a dream of surgical instruments may be insignificant.

insult Were you the victim, or the propagator, of the insult? If the victim, by the mechanism of contraries you can expect significant praise to follow. If you perpetrated an insult, be especially careful to give praise where praise is due, and not to take all the credit for successful projects, at work or at home.

interruption If, in your dreams, your tasks are repeatedly interrupted, this can signal serious obstacles in your path to achieving a goal. A period of frustration is likely, possibly even a major reversal.

iron *See* metals.

island Especially if you are stressed, this can indicate the need to take time out to nourish your sense of self and contemplate your life. Possibly you would benefit from a period of isolation. If this cannot be managed, try taking up meditation or some other relaxation therapy.

itching This can signal that meeting some unfulfilled, possibly unrecognized, desire, would be of great benefit to your mental health. Try to identify such desires and form an action plan for bringing them to fruition.

J
. . . .

jackpot By the mechanism of contraries, to dream of winning the jackpot can indicate a financial loss. If you dream of someone else winning a jackpot, expect generosity from some unexpected quarter.

jagged edges Dreams of jagged rocks, or jagged knives, can indicate that you need to take precaution against fire and flood.

jargon Do you understand the jargon, or not? If your dream features highly technical jargon that you use in your everyday life, this could be a neutral symbol. If it features jargon you do not normally use, or even fully understand, expect to do battle with a major opponent, such as a big corporation, a powerful individual, or an entire system. You may have to travel to put across your side of the story and may attract a good deal of unwelcome publicity.

jealousy What is the role of jealousy in your waking life? You cannot understand the role of jealousy in a dream until you are clear on this point. In general, by the mechanism of contraries, dreams of jealousy can indicate that this emotion is inappropriate in your waking life – you can expect fidelity in your sexual and family relationships, from your colleagues, etc.

jellyfish Jellyfish can be a symbol of uncertainty in any sphere. Do not be overconfident. If you think you know all the answers to a problem, you are probably a long way from solving it. Jellyfish can also symbolize wisdom and wise counsel.

jewellery The meaning of the dream will depend, in part, on the type of jewellery – necklace, brooch, earrings, etc. – on whether it is costume jewellery or not and on the type of stones it contains. The meaning will also change for men and for women, and for those who wear or own a lot of jewellery and those who do not. In general, though, dreams of jewellery can herald periods of financial hardship and can be warnings against being led astray by vanity and the desire to show off. *See also* Precious stones and gems.

joker To dream of a joker, juggler, jester, or similar figure, is a warning not to allow yourself to hide fears, worries, concerns, etc. under a laughing façade. You may be able to fool others, but not yourself, and if you do not confront darker emotions, your mental health will suffer, as may your relationships, career, etc.

jokes What was the nature of the joke and who was the joker? You will need to think about issues such as these before attempting an interpretation. But, by the mechanism of contraries, dream jokes often have a darker meaning, perhaps indicating trouble in the area featured in the joke – sex, business or whatever.

journey Is the journey welcome, or not? Is it trouble free, or fraught with difficulty? What is the mode of transport? You will need to consider questions such as these before attempting an interpretation, but, in general, dreams of journeys can presage waking travel. They can also signal change of all sorts, welcome and unwelcome, important and trivial, long term and short term, etc. *See also* Geographical dreams.

joy You may be able to accept the dream at face value, but remember that, by the mechanism of contraries, this could indicate sadness to come.

judgement/judges If you are involved in the legal profession, this may be a neutral symbol for you, reflecting your everyday concerns. For others, any dream featuring aspects of the justice system may be highly significant. Are you involved in perpetrating some injustice, perhaps via your work? Do you flout the law? If so, why? Questions such as these are likely to help you interpret dreams of judges and judgement, as they mostly concern your own guilt.

jug This can be a dream about your household finances and resources. A period of belt tightening could be called for: you need to take care of what you already have; saving and maintaining should be your watchwords, not squandering and gaining. *See also* kettle.

juggling If you dream of watching a juggler, you should be warned that someone is trying to deceive you. If you dream of juggling, it suggests that some act of deception on your part is about to be uncovered. Do you have a guilty conscience? If so, it could be time to own up.

jumping This can be a dream about overcoming obstacles. With a bit of exertion, you can overcome most problems to reach your ends.

jungle This can be a dream about the role of spiritual forces in your life. Do not neglect the life of the spirit. Alternatively, it can be a dream predicting obstacles in your path, hinting that you will achieve your ends only after considerable effort, much of it intellectual, not physical. Or again, it could be a prod from your subconscious, telling you to husband your financial resources and start recycling.

jury Dreams of juries often concern the need for independence of spirit, or the need to resist being swayed by the opinions of others. You are being told to weigh evidence carefully before making a decision, and to go with your own beliefs and opinions, not attitudes imposed on you by others.

K

kettle This can have meanings similar to jug, but it has an added dimension concerning your grace as a host or hostess. If you dream of a dirty or broken kettle, perhaps others perceive you as unwelcoming or mean. If you dream of a well-kept kettle, others probably perceive you as warm and welcoming, and your home as a good place to be.

keyhole If you dream about being spied upon, or spying through a keyhole, it could be a warning of possible treachery. You could also be being prodded into opening up to new possibilities and into looking for important messages from unexpected quarters.

keys A single key can be an unlucky symbol in a dream, especially if it is dropped, becomes stuck in a lock, or is broken. A bunch of keys can symbolize authority. In some circumstances, any type of key or key ring could presage a house move, possibly unexpected and in the near future.

kick Dreams of kicking, whether by humans or animals, and whether you are the one kicked or the one doing the kicking, tend to be about competition and your reaction to it. If you are naturally aggressive, take this as a hint that you should modify your aggression; if you lack assertiveness, take it as a hint that you need to make your needs known more clearly or risk being trampled.

kidnap For parents, a dream that their child has been kidnapped can be a straightforward expression of anxiety. Otherwise, kidnapping can be a symbol of consumption. To dream of being kidnapped oneself can be a symbol of the need for financial prudence and the need to protect your property. To dream of kidnapping someone else can be a warning against greed and overreaching ambition. To dream about a kidnapping in which you have no personal involvement can be a symbol of the need to be careful with resources that do not belong to you – for example, your company's resources or environmental resources.

Kissing

What was the nature of the kiss? One you sought and enjoyed, or not? Are you in a relationship, or not? This is the sort of consideration that should influence your interpretation, but, in general, a dream of kissing means good things are on the way. A dream that you are kissing a child can be a sign that you will succeed in some venture. A dream that you are watching two children exchange a sweet kiss could mean that someone close to you will succeed in some venture – if you have teenage children, it could mean that either you or your parents will soon receive an unexpected financial gain (unhappily, it does *not* mean that you are about to come into your parents' riches!). If you are single, a dream of kissing someone could be a divinatory dream – you could be about to meet that person.

killing What sort of killing was it? Human or animal? Were you personally involved, even the perpetrator – or the victim? You need to think about factors such as this before attempting an interpretation. Also remember that the mechanism of contraries may be at work – this may be a dream about beginning a new life, rather than ending a life. Whatever the exact details, dreams of killing are nearly always significant. Symbolic interpretations range from a warning against killing with kindness, to warnings against killing aspects of yourself.

king A dream of a king can be concerned with healing – emotional, physical or spiritual. It can also be concerned with protection, especially of babies and children.

kitchen If you work in, or spend much of your time in, a kitchen, this could be a neutral symbol, reflecting your daily activities. For others, it might be a symbol of domestic security, or its lack. A well-kept kitchen, with a pleasant atmosphere, can symbolize domestic harmony. A dirty, ill-kept kitchen can symbolize domestic discord.

kite Did the kite fly easily, or not? Were you flying it alone, or with others, especially children? If you were flying the kite with others and it rose easily into the sky, expect to be able to fulfil your immediate ambitions. If you were flying it alone, and could not get it to rise, expect trouble ahead.

kitten The meaning will change depending on your circumstances, but this can symbolize a romantic affair with disastrous consequences.

knight The knight can be an archetypal figure of honour and traditional values. In your waking life, are you on the brink of behaving dishonourably? If so, think hard about the possible consequences and your inevitable feelings of guilt.

knitting If you knit as a hobby, this may be a neutral symbol reflecting your everyday activities. If you rarely, or never, knit, consider various questions before attempting an interpretation. Were you knitting or watching someone else knitting? What was being knitted? Was the knitter skilled, or not? A skilled knitter, working on an intricate pattern, can indicate that the solution to a problem that has been troubling you will soon present itself. An unskilled knitter, who continually drops stitches, etc., can indicate that you are avoiding difficult problems, which will soon become pressing.

knives If you dream of receiving a knife as a present, expect a long-standing friendship to be broken quickly. To dream of finding a knife is an unlucky omen. If you dream of a knife lying on the ground, or sharp edge up on a table, beware of giving unintended offence to others. If you dream of a knife being knocked from a table, expect a stranger to come into your life. If you dream of a knife just before embarking on an important journey in your waking life, your travels will go smoothly. If you dream of stirring a cup of liquid with a knife, expect rows and trouble at home.

knocking To hear knockings in your dream can be an omen of grief to follow.

knots This dream can have different meanings for men and for women, and for those who wish to conceive a child and those who do not. In either sex, to dream of tying or untying knots can be linked to one's desire to, and chances of, conceiving a child – difficulty in untying a knot can indicate difficulty in conception. For women of childbearing age, especially those who are pregnant, dreams of knots can be connected with anxiety about childbirth. Dreams of knots can also be connected with your deep thoughts about the afterlife – only you will be able to work out the meaning of dreams that suggest this context. Knots can also be a lucky symbol of protection and cure.

L
. . . .

laboratory If you work in a laboratory, this may be a neutral symbol reflecting your everyday experience. For others, it symbolizes intellectual effort, especially co-operative, team effort. Your dream could be telling you that you need to accept the ideas and suggestions of others, if you are to make progress on a problem.

lace If lace appears in your dream, take it as a warning that you need to pay more attention to nitty-gritty detail, and not just the big picture, when making decisions or trying to solve problems. You must try to develop patience and persistence.

ladder Were you climbing the ladder, or coming down? Were you carrying a ladder, standing on a ladder while painting a house, walking under a ladder... or what? You must think about all these things before attempting an interpretation, and also about the condition of the ladder and what it was made of. In general, to climb up a ladder suggests the fulfilment of some ambition; to climb down a ladder suggests disappointment, especially financial disappointment. Depending on your personal circumstances, a dream of a ladder may signify trouble in a romantic relationship, possibly even the cancellation of a wedding. *See also* the discussion of Freud in Chapter 7.

landslide A landslide can signify reversal of your fortunes, either for better or for worse. In either case, the changes will occur despite any actions or attempted actions on your part.

laughter By the mechanism of contraries, laughter in a dream can sometimes herald grief and tears. But if your dream was of children laughing, that is always a positive sign of hope.

leather To dream of hides, or leather bags, shoes, belts, etc. can be a sign of good luck coming to your home or business – especially if you are self-employed. If you are unwell, leather can symbolize a return to good health.

leaves Dreams of catching falling leaves, or of leaves blowing into your house, are unlucky portents. If you are single, and dream of leaves, this can suggest that you will soon find a new partner.

leprechaun *See* fairy.

letter Did you write the letter, or receive it? Did you place it in the post box? Was it written on plain paper, or fancy, coloured paper? You must think about questions such as these before reaching any conclusions but, in general, a letter is a fairly transparent symbol about the relationship between the sender and the receiver. This dream is telling you to expect important news, but only you can determine what the nature of this news is likely to be. Junk mail has a different meaning; it is telling you not to allow yourself to be bogged down in trivialities. To dream of dropping a letter, of any sort, can herald bad luck in the area with which the letter was concerned – romance, business, etc. *See also* message.

lightning Lightning can be a message from your subconscious that you need to become more accepting in your approach to problems, more focused and more grounded. It can also be a symbol of good luck to come and of danger averted.

lights, lanterns and torches Dreams of sources of light, such as lanterns, lights and torches, can foretell an unexpected and traumatic loss of property, possibly involving violence. However, they can also foretell light at the end of the tunnel – you will soon solve some problem that has been troubling you, or emerge from a period of unhappiness to tranquillity. To witness a light going out can suggest that you are paying insufficient attention to your spiritual life – light can be an archetypal symbol of spirituality and enlightenment. Lasers as light sources can indicate violence – *see* Louise's dream, Chapter 3, for lasers.

limping If you dream of watching somebody with a limp, it could mean that you will soon be called upon to help somebody through trouble. If you dream of an animal limping, it could mean that you are about to take on a new pet – perhaps a rescue dog? If you yourself are limping, a period of listlessness and tiredness might be about to befall you.

litter/litter bin A dream of litter, of litter-strewn places, or of a litter bin, can indicate that you are much too preoccupied with petty detail. Relax!

locks Dreams of locks, especially of difficulty in opening locks, can indicate that you are soon to become embroiled in lengthy negotiations, possibly over contracts or other legal or quasi-legal issues.

loss By the mechanism of contraries, to dream of a loss often indicates a gain.

lottery If numbers are revealed to you in your dream, you should at least consider using them next time you play. Do not be surprised if dreams of a big win are not followed up by success in the waking world – the mechanism of contraries could be at work.

luggage If you are about to take a journey, or have recently returned from one, this could be a neutral symbol reflecting your recent experiences. For others, dreams of luggage can be telling you to be prepared for all eventualities, and to start planning and preparing now for major changes.

luxury The meaning of this dream will change depending on your waking attitude to luxury and the quality of your life. Among those who live in luxury, dreams of luxury can be a way of showing them how lucky they are and a warning against taking luxury for granted, or falling into greed or selfishness. For those who live in reduced circumstances, these can be classic wish-fulfilment dreams, or may contain clues for action plans about improving their conditions. *See* Louise's dreams, Chapter 3.

lying It is almost impossible to offer firm guidelines. The meaning of a dream in which you are lying depends largely on your waking attitude to the truth, how truthful you have been recently, whether you feel guilty about lies told now or in the past. Are you being told to confront some guilt and make amends? A dream in which you are lied to could be a simple warning not to take others at face value, or it could carry wider meanings about the role of honesty and dishonesty in your life.

M

mail van To dream of a mail van can indicate a wish come true.

man Are you male or female? What did the man do and what did he look like? You need to consider issues such as these before attempting an interpretation. Often, a single man – previously unknown to you – can stand for mankind in general, so this could be a political dream, calling you to wake up to some global problem or terrible injustice, and to do what you can to help. Alternatively, it could be a dream about the importance of the masculine in your life – whether you are male or female. *See also* woman.

map Maps can concern literal travel in a straightforward way. But they can also symbolize spiritual travel and guidance in reaching some desired destination – literal or metaphorical. *See also* Geographical dreams.

marriage Are you married, or not? Are you divorced? Are you male or female? All these factors must be taken into account when deciding on an interpretation, as must the nature of the wedding you witnessed. Did the bride and groom seem happy? Was it a traditional ceremony, or not? Were there lots of guests, or not? By the mechanism of contraries, a dream of a marriage does not always herald happiness, but to dream of actually touching the bride or groom generally augurs well. At a metaphysical level, dreams of marriage can concern balance between opposing forces, or properties, acting in your life or personality.

married man/married woman To dream of a married man, if you are female, or a married woman, if male, can be a straightforward warning against temptation, or getting involved in an inappropriate relationship.

measuring The meaning of dreams of measuring, and counting and weighing, depends largely on what is being measured, counted or weighed. To measure a child for clothes suggests a life of poverty and hardship; to measure yourself for clothes suggests you will not be getting any new ones in the short term. To dream of measuring out wool, cotton or string can indicate a cure for illness. In general, counting in a dream suggests financial loss and weighing, especially weighing food, suggests continued financial difficulties.

meat For vegetarians, a dream of meat will probably carry political overtones. For others, to dream of buying meat indicates that you will soon find the solution to a long-standing problem, but to dream of cooking meat can be a sign of ill luck. To dream of carving and eating meat can mean that your social world is about to expand in interesting ways. To dream of throwing meat away is a warning against wastefulness and overconsumption of all types. If you have such a dream, why not start recycling all your rubbish, if you do not already do so? For a butcher, a dream of meat can be a neutral symbol, reflecting everyday activities.

melting To dream of things melting – ice, ice cream, chocolate, etc. – can indicate the gradual erosion of your self-confidence and the necessity to take immediate steps to confront whatever it is that is causing this erosion – a bad relationship, an unsympathetic boss, a large weight gain, or whatever. Only you can decide on appropriate action.

Metals

A dream of metal needs to be interpreted in the light of your personal circumstances and the context of the dream. The condition of the metal is important. Is it an ore? Is it shiny, or dull? Is it being used for something (e.g. to manufacture cars)? Is it a precious metal? When answering questions such as these, it is worth bearing in mind that metals can symbolize our moral attitudes. Note that it is possible to give only cursory meanings here; much will depend on specific details of your dream.
Precious metals: these stand for honourable courses of action. You should think through any difficult moral problems in order to reach your own conclusions. **Lead:** you are soon likely to be caught in a moral quagmire. **Copper:** do not allow yourself to be used as a conduit for spreading prejudiced beliefs. **Iron:** do not be tempted by violent solutions. Dreams of mining metal ores can be concerned with the need to keep searching for the truth, even if it is elusive.

mending To dream of mending that which is broken indicates that something currently not broken will soon break. This could refer to a literal breaking – for example, your car could break down, or your central heating, but is as likely to refer to relationship breakdown, at home or at work.

mermaid A symbol of temptation that you must resist, for your own safety.

message To dream of sending or receiving a message (a memo, a voicemail) could, by the mechanism of contraries, indicate that all your lines of communication are about to be messed up. This could be literal – your phone lines go down, your email crashes – or it could be metaphorical: there are misunderstandings between you and those you love or those you work with. A message can also indicate that you must listen to what those in authority over you have to say – bite your tongue if you have to. *See also* letter.

midnight To hear a clock strike midnight in your dream indicates that you are entering a fruitful period where all things are possible for you. Take advantage of all the opportunities currently opening up.

milk To dream of spilling milk is unlucky and can indicate loss of property. To dream of giving someone milk to drink is a lucky symbol and can indicate domestic happiness.

mirror To dream of breaking a mirror indicates extreme bad luck. To dream of a covered mirror can indicate coming ill health. Otherwise, the meaning of the dream depends largely on what you saw in the mirror. To see yourself reflected can indicate the need to be on your guard against deceit. To see a baby or child indicates a happiness. To see more than one person can indicate a quarrel ahead. To see a stranger indicates that one will soon enter your life, with important, possibly romantic, consequences. To see animals can mean bad luck.

mist *See* fog.

mistress A woman dreaming that her partner has a mistress is a clear sign that all is not well in her relationship. If a faithful man dreams that he has a mistress, it carries the same meaning. If an unfaithful man dreams of his mistress, this may be of no significance, from a dream interpretation point of view.

money As you would expect, dreams of money concern financial success, or lack of it. Always be aware that the mechanism of contraries might be operating. For example, to dream of a big monetary gain could herald a loss. To dream of dropping coins indicates temporary financial difficulties. To dream of an empty pocket or purse indicates longer-term financial difficulty. To find money and keep it indicates coming bad luck, usually of a physical nature (e.g. you might suffer a minor injury). If you dream of finding money and then giving it away, the ill luck will be averted.

months *See* seasonable/unseasonable.

moon The meaning will depend on the details of the dream and on your personal circumstances. Are you male or female? In either case, a dream of the moon can concern the role of the feminine and intuitive in your nature. Often, dreams of the moon concern the timing of new enterprises. To dream of the new moon suggests that this is a good time to start new enterprises, especially business enterprises. To dream of the waning moon suggests that your timing is not so good. The full moon suggests the best time of all. To dream of undertaking some enterprise in moonlight suggests that the enterprise will fail. It is unlucky to dream of pointing at the moon.

morning If your dream is set in the morning, you will soon find something you had given up for lost.

mother Are you male or female? Is your mother alive or dead? What is, or was, the tone of your relationship with her? Are you yourself a parent? Considerations such as these will influence your thinking but, in general, to dream of your mother can be a reference to the nurturing, protective and creative side of yourself. *See also* father.

mountain To dream of a mountain, especially climbing a mountain, can symbolize that, after much effort and hardship, you will overcome obstacles in your path and attain some ambition, possibly connected with spiritual growth – you will be granted a new perspective on the world.

mud A dream of mud can be a warning against abusing your health. For example, it could be a warning against overindulgence in food or alcohol, or you could be being given a coded message about the importance of quitting smoking. Muddy water can indicate confused thinking about your body, perhaps about your sexuality.

N

....

nagging Were you nagging, or being nagged? In waking life, do you have a reputation for nagging? Factors such as these will influence your interpretation. But, as a guide, these dreams are about facing resentment, rather than letting it fester. If you dream of doing the nagging yourself, your subconscious is trying to nag you into recognizing, and dealing with, some underlying resentment. If you were being nagged, you are being warned that someone has a suppressed resentment towards you. Try to identify who and what this might be, and face the problem head on.

nails Finger- and toenails can be a sign that someone wishes you ill. A manicure or pedicure can indicate the need to moderate the image you project to the world. If you are sick, to dream of hammering in metal nails indicates that you will soon be cured. If you are in good health, it can indicate that the solution to a problem will soon present itself. If you dream of metal nails lying about on the floor, that is an omen of ill luck to come.

nakedness Dreams about being naked in a public place are common anxiety dreams, reflecting our concern about our social standing and the way others perceive us – your subconscious is addressing issues of honour and shame. Dreams of being naked can also indicate your need, or desire, to be freed from constriction, the literal constriction of clothes and social constrictions that govern our behaviour in public. Of course, you should remember that some desires are exciting only when confined to the dream world – do not take such a dream as a licence to go naked in the street!

names To dream of your own name being called is a warning to be on your guard against those with malicious intentions towards you. To hear another name being called can have a variety of meanings, but probably someone with this name will be significant in your life, for good or ill. To dream of forgetting your own name is a warning not to let others presume upon you, or take you for granted. To dream of asking whether someone knows who you are is a sign of pride.

needle To dream of a needle breaking while you are using it signifies either that you will receive news from a distant relative regarding a legacy, or that the wearer of the clothes you are making will receive such news. To dream of dropping a needle and not picking it up suggests you are in for some bad luck.

neighbours The nature of this dream depends entirely on your relationship with your neighbours and only you can determine its exact meaning. To dream of a row with your neighbours can herald a row in waking life. Sometimes a dream of your neighbours indicates that either you, or they, will soon be moving house.

net A dream of a net may reflect a fear of confinement, or, by the mechanism of contraries, it may indicate that you are about to win new freedoms – maybe you will be offered increased responsibility at work? Dreams of nets may also indicate financial entanglements, and a need to sort out your finances, perhaps by clearing debt.

news It does not matter if you dream of watching the news on television, listening to it on the radio, or reading the newspaper. In all cases the interpretation depends on the nature of the news. If it is gloomy, do not be alarmed: the mechanism of contraries could be at work. Alternatively, it could be prodding you into taking your duties as a citizen more seriously, or into thinking more seriously about international issues. For all of us, items from the news sometimes intrude into our dreams in a neutral way, just because they have been discussed that day.

night If your dream has a night-time setting, be prepared for setbacks, especially those involving loss of important personal papers – driving licence, passport, etc.

noise Dream noises related to actual noises – the alarm clock going off, a car alarm wailing in the street – are irrelevant. If, in your dreams, you hear peculiar noises that cannot be explained in the usual ways, expect family rows, especially if you have adolescent children.

Numbers

How do you use numbers in your waking life? Are you good at maths, or maths phobic? You will need to answer these questions before attempting any interpretation but, in general, numbers stand for mystical beauty and the power of the abstract. They can also represent time, as in Joseph's dream – *see* Chapter 8. You may disagree with the interpretations offered for the numbers 0 to 10; if so, use your dream diary as a springboard for figuring out what numbers mean in your dreams: **0** – absence and absences of all sorts; **1** – unity in any context; **2** – polarity in any context; **3** – unfathomable mystery; **4** – regularity and balance; **5** – a symbol of isolation; **6** – creativity all its manifestations; **7** – the power of the non-rational; **8** – evolution and progression; **9** – initiation; **10** – perfection.

nomad A dream of a nomadic figure – a tribesman roaming from pasture to pasture – may indicate that you are oppressed by your environment, and that a change of scenery would do you good.

nonsense words If you hear unintelligible nonsense words in your dreams, you are being warned against too easily and mistakenly accepting obvious explanations for problems, without investigating all the other possibilities. Try to be more critical in your thinking.

noon/midday If your dream is set at noon, you must be especially careful to keep a clear head and think rationally. To dream of eating at midday can symbolize that others are trying to con you.

nurse If you are a nurse, this can be a neutral symbol reflecting your everyday activities. For others, the dream can signify happiness in personal and family relationships.

nursery Do you have children, or not? Do you want children, or not? Such questions should influence your interpretation of this dream, but often dreams of a nursery have a positive meaning, suggesting success in new ventures, travel or business.

nuts For the single, nuts can indicate that they will soon be involved in a new relationship. For a woman of childbearing age, nuts can symbolize that she will soon become pregnant.

O

oasis This symbolizes literal and metaphorical refuge. Are you in need of refuge, or could you offer it to others?

oath Did you witness someone swearing an oath, or take one yourself? If you witnessed someone else taking an oath, then you are in line for promotion at work. If you took the oath yourself, someone will soon consult you about an issue of which you have only sketchy knowledge. Be very careful what you say.

obesity The meaning of such a dream changes according to whether or not you need to lose weight. If you do need to lose weight, it could be a simple anxiety dream, or an anxiety dream combined with a hint to form an action plan to tackle your weight problem. If you do not need to lose weight, a dream of obesity may be warning you to take care of what you have, recognize when enough is enough and guard against waste.

obituary Who was the obituary for? How many details can you remember? The answers to such questions will help shape your interpretation. In general, a dream of an obituary need not herald gloomy news, because of the mechanism of contraries. To dream of your own obituary could be your subconscious's way of telling you that you are unnecessarily doing yourself down, selling yourself short or otherwise acting too much like a doormat.

obsession The dream obsession will probably reflect a waking obsession. Your subconscious is emphasizing the necessity of confronting and dealing with this obsession, so that you can return to peace of mind.

ocean What were the conditions out in the ocean? Calm? Choppy? Very rough? You cannot interpret this symbol without considering factors such as these. But, in general, such dreams concern courage. You are being told that you have the courage to face and overcome problems, or are being exhorted to show courage, or congratulated on recent displays of courage.

offence *See* insult.

office Do you work in an office? If so, this dream will have different meanings for you than for those who do not. Often, office dreams reflect unhappiness with your job. If you find yourself working in an unfamiliar office, or doing unfamiliar work, this is a warning that others have spotted that you are not pulling your weight and are not performing to expected standards. Dreams about your colleagues are often about trust and loyalty, but you can interpret them only in the light of your actual relationships.

ogre Your subconscious is trying to tell you that some activity, practice or interest of yours is doing you actual harm, physical, emotional or spiritual. This could be anything from smoking to taking drugs, to forcing someone else to fulfil your sexual desires, to petty crime to habitual lying. Try to identify the activity causing problems and take action to control it. Get professional help, if need be.

oil There are many types of oil – cooking oil, massage oil and the black stuff that comes out of the ground. Cooking oil often indicates domestic happiness; massage oil can indicate dissatisfaction with your sensual life and trouble in romantic relationships. The black stuff can be a symbol of overconsumption of all sorts and carries a warning to cut down on waste.

openings Open doors, open pits in the ground, open boxes, open vessels, and so on, can all indicate that you are about to meet a boundary in your life, and must think seriously about the implications of crossing it. By the mechanism of contraries, open graves can indicate good luck to come.

opera Can you remember which opera you saw? Did you enjoy it, or not? If not, you are skilled at seeing through deception and artifice and are not easily led astray by sumptuous displays of wealth. If yes, you need to be on your guard against falsity and deception, and be willing to take a more critical attitude to outward appearances.

operation For a surgeon or a nurse, such a dream is probably insignificant. For others, it is important to note whether you were being operated on, or doing the operation. If you were being operated on, you need to develop a more trusting approach to others, and be willing to sacrifice your individuality to work as part of a team. If you were doing the operation, you need to guard against allowing others to build up a falsely flattering opinion of you.

opposites It is always lucky to dream of a member of the opposite sex. Apart from this, dreams of opposites often concern the need for balance and harmony in our lives, and the desirability of considering a variety of perspectives.

orchard To dream of an orchard indicates that you have become stuck in a rut, or stuck in old ways. You need to cultivate new interests, read new books, visit new places and generally give your mental life a boost.

orchestra This dream will have different meanings for musicians than for the rest of us. For musicians, it may be an insignificant dream. For others, an orchestra can symbolize coming turmoil and the temporary need to avoid drawing the attention of others, to keep one's head down and try to get on with life.

orchid To dream of an orchid flower can symbolize fragility – perhaps of a relationship.

orgy A dream of an orgy can indicate that you know full well you must exercise restraint in your life, but are having some difficulty admitting this to yourself.

P

pain By the mechanism of contraries, to dream of pain often indicates that some nagging pain will shortly disappear. Alternatively, it can be a warning to take the pain seriously and consult a doctor, before your condition deteriorates.

paint/painting Dreams of paint and painting often represent creativity – sometimes a creativity that is being denied expression. A dream of paint in a pot can indicate dissatisfaction in some area of your life. Paintbrushes or rollers can mean you are rising to the challenge of such dissatisfaction. For the significance of paint colours, *see* colour. If you dream that you are painting a room, this can indicate that you lack security in your life, and must take steps to avoid people who would exploit you. If you dream of watching someone else paint a room, you should learn to trust someone about whom you have harboured doubts. If you dream that you are viewing a painting, or are wandering around an art gallery, this can indicate that your creativity is being stifled, or that your ambitions to stretch yourself intellectually are being thwarted. If you dream that you are painting a picture, this can mean that your creativity is about to be given full rein. If you dream that you are watching someone else paint a picture, this might mean that you will soon help somebody else achieve his or her creative ambitions.

parents *See* father, mother.

park To dream of visiting a park, especially with children, can symbolize happiness and innocence. *See* Mary's dream, Chapter 5.

parties *See* Louise's dream, Chapter 3, for a full analysis.

parting To dream of a parting often heralds a significant meeting. To dream of parting at a gate can herald bad luck, as can saying goodbye more than once. If you dream of watching someone until they are out of sight, this can mean you will never see that person again.

pearls To dream of pearls can mean tears are coming.

pens Pens can be a symbol of greed for money and all sorts of material possessions. Do you have a problem with greed? Do you need to sit down and think about when enough is enough? To dream of writing can be a hint that you should try to become clear in your own mind about some problem affecting your family life, marriage or children.

pets If you are a pet owner, dreaming of your pet indicates that you need to deal with some significant stress in your life before it starts to have a serious detrimental effect on your wellbeing.

photograph/photographer If you dream of having your photograph taken, that can foretell a period of ill health. If you are a sportsman or sportswoman, it can foretell a period when you are off form and cannot maintain your usual level of performance. If you dream of taking a photograph, you are being warned to examine your own motives towards someone close to you – are you misleading them, or do you secretly wish them ill? To dream of black-and-white photographs suggests the importance of seeing both sides of an argument. Unless you are a photographer, to dream of a photographer means you are at risk of falling under someone else's bad influence.

If you are a photographer, dreams of photographs and photographers are probably insignificant.

pies Pies are a very lucky sign, indicating that your life will be filled with good things, good friends and good health.

pillars You can expect to be embroiled in a far-ranging controversy, possibly legal in nature.

pins The context is most important, as pins can represent a variety of factors. Dreams of rusty pins often foretell broken friendships; shiny pins suggest a new friendship. Sometimes pins warn of powerful forces working against you, even supernatural forces. If you dream of finding a pin, expect a financial windfall, possibly through gambling. If you dreamed of seeing a pin on the ground and not picking it up, expect a financial loss. If you are single, dreams of pins can foretell a new relationship. If you are sick, they can herald a return to health. If you are about to undertake a long journey, a dream of pins can be a warning to delay your travel plans.

pipes Plumbing pipes and gas pipes etc. tend to be hints from your subconscious that you should take a more optimistic view of life and try to be more positive in your thinking. They can also have sexual connotations. If you work with pipes in your daily life (e.g. if you are a plumber), such dreams are likely to be insignificant. Tobacco pipes can suggest that you are failing to meet some obligation, and you should take appropriate action.

planets The planets, taken as a group, symbolize wandering. This may be taken literally to mean a pleasant country stroll with no particular aim, or aimless spiritual wandering. Try to determine the direction of your life if you dream of a planet, and think about how to get back on track if you have lost your way.

plates To dream of plates can herald unhappiness connected with your domestic pets, even their death.

police If you are a member of the police, such dreams are unlikely to be significant. For others, much depends on your prior dealings with the police. If you have ever been arrested, your dream could reflect guilt, remorse, bitterness, resentment or whatever. If you have always had positive dealings with the police, such a dream may indicate that some area of your personality is in need of protection or, alternatively, of being arrested (i.e. curbed). For parents, such a dream may indicate that you are being under- or overprotective towards children.

Precious stones and gems

You can interpret dreams of precious gems only in the light of your own circumstances and experience, especially in the light of your own financial standing. The condition of the gemstone, whether it is cut, in a fancy setting, loose on a cloth, etc. is important, as is its colour. But, in general, gems often have a dual symbolism, representing issues connected with bodily health, and also inherent value. Note that it is possible to give only cursory meanings here; much will depend on specific details of your dream. **Diamond:** indicates your indomitable spirit and ability to stand up to attack, or powerful modern medicines. **Amethyst:** purification and peace, or the need to expel poisons from the body. **Emerald:** sight and blindness, literal and metaphorical. **Ruby:** rationality and clear thinking, or the need for bodily warmth. **Sapphire:** protection from evil influences, or from skin diseases. Substances that began as living things, such as amber or coral, are often counted as gems. Their significance will be moderated by their source; for example, amber, which is fossilized pine-tree resin, may symbolize calming of the nerves, which is also symbolized by forests. *See also* jewellery.

postman/woman A postman/woman in your dream can represent exciting new possibilities that will shortly open up for you, and, more straightforwardly, that you will soon receive important news.

praise If, in your dreams, you are being given extravagant praise, by the mechanism of contraries beware of people trying to undermine your reputation, or blame you unjustly for some problem. If you are praising another, especially if you are in a managerial position, this could be a hint that you are too stinting with your praise to colleagues and that your team would benefit if you could praise more readily.

prams, pushchairs and strollers If a woman of childbearing age dreams of pushing an empty baby carriage, she might soon find herself pregnant.

pregnancy This dream has different meanings for older and younger women, and women and men. Often, a dream of pregnancy is connected with an actual pregnancy or, metaphorically, with the creation of something new and precious. If this is not the case, dreams of pregnancy can be warnings against adultery or other inappropriate sexual liaisons. *See also* Chapters 7 and 8.

presents If you dream of receiving abundant presents, expect a financial loss. If you dream of giving presents, expect a gain. If you dreamed of giving Christmas presents at any time other than Christmas, this is an unlucky portent. If you dream of receiving birthday presents at any time other than your birthday, this is also unlucky.

prism A prism can indicate that you need to give your imagination full rein and follow your dreams.

prison Were you yourself imprisoned? If so, for a long or short period of time? A long imprisonment suggests long-term obstacles to reaching a goal; a shorter imprisonment suggests shorter-term problems. If you dream of seeing others imprisoned, that can suggest you need to analyse problems carefully and try to see all sides of an argument. The condition of the prison is also significant. If it is clean and modern, that can suggest that you are worrying unnecessarily about something; a dirty, overcrowded prison can suggest that you ought to be worrying about something you currently regard as trivial.

pudding For those in relationships, a beautifully prepared and presented pudding can be a sign of happiness, while a pudding that falls apart in the cooking or on the plate can symbolize discord. For the single, well-prepared puddings indicate that a happy new relationship will soon begin; a collapsed pudding indicates that you should be wary of entering a new relationship.

punishment Were you the one being punished, or handing out the punishment, or were you merely a witness to some punishment? If you were being punished, your subconscious is trying to get you to confront some long-suppressed guilt. If you were handing out the punishment, you probably need to adopt a more compassionate approach to someone over

whom you have control (e.g. someone who works for you).
If you were a witness to punishment, you can expect to be
consulted on some quasi-legal matter. If, in your dreams, the
punishment vastly outweighed the supposed crime, the issues
referred to are much more important than you at first think.

pyramid A pyramid can be a symbol of the role of secrecy and
mystery in your life. It can also symbolize the afterlife.

Q

quarantine If you dream of an animal being placed in
quarantine, that is a straightforward message that you will
soon be undertaking foreign travel – even if you do not have
a pet. If you dream of being placed in quarantine for some
reason, then it is possible that some aspect of your personality
is doing you active harm and you should try to moderate it.
If you dream of visiting someone in quarantine, you are being
encouraged to work on identifying and confronting deep-
seated fears.

quarrels If you have recently had a major row, such a dream
is unlikely to be significant. Otherwise, by the mechanism of
contraries, to dream of quarrels signifies their absence and
you can expect a peaceful few weeks.

quarry Unless you work in a quarry, such a dream is likely to
symbolize obstacles in your path to success and that you need
to work hard to extract all you can from every possibility and
opportunity that presents itself to you.

quarters If you dream of something – a cake, an orange, an
amount of money – being divided into four, this can mean
that you are about to undergo an unpleasant experience – but
it will be short, and insignificant in the long run.

queen This is a straightforward symbol of tradition, whose
meaning will depend on whether you are a monarchist or a
republican. For monarchists, a dream of a queen is liable to
symbolize the comforts and security of tradition, while for
republicans such a dream is liable to emphasize the repressive,
unthinking and stifling aspects of tradition. Dreams of kings,
princes and princesses all have roughly the same meaning. For
dreams featuring embarrassing social encounters with royalty,

see the entry on nakedness, as the two types of dream have much the same function.

questionnaire This can be a symbol of your dealings with the state and officialdom. Such dreams are often asking you to think about your role and duties as a citizen (e.g. with respect to paying taxes, voting, etc.). Alternatively, such dreams can reflect deep dissatisfaction with the political status quo.

questions If you are lucky, your dream will contain questions that it will be fruitful for you to ask in your waking life, and which will suggest new approaches and avenues of enquiry. If you dream of being questioned, you are being encouraged to adopt a questioning attitude. If you dream of questioning another, you are being encouraged to listen to the experts, but not necessarily to take what they say at face value.

queue Patience, diligence and attention to detail are required if you are to solve a problem.

quicksand If you dreamed of sinking in quicksand, you are probably being warned against exhaustion and trying to juggle too many commitments. Can you drop any commitments for the sake of your mental health? If you witness someone sinking in quicksand, you are being encouraged to think through how you might help others shed some of their commitments.

quilt This signifies that you are about to enter a creative period and it is a good time to take up artistic pursuits. If you want to write a novel, start now! If you want to paint, or write songs, start now! If you enjoy crafts, cookery or gardening, then this dream is telling you that now is a good time to undertake an important new project.

quivering If you dream that you are quivering, or that you are watching another person or an animal quivering, this is generally an omen of bad news to come.

quizzes To dream of a quiz can indicate that, after a period of mutual suspicion, you will shortly make a new friend who will widen your social horizons considerably.

R

. . . .

race What sort of race was it? A car race, horse race or running race? Were you participating, or merely a spectator? Such considerations will influence your interpretation but, in general, races of all sorts signify your competitive, aggressive spirit. Depending on your personal circumstances, it could be telling you that you would benefit from being either more or less competitive. If, before a big sporting event, you dream of the result, it might be worth taking your dream seriously and laying a bet. *See* Chapter 8.

rackets/racket games This can mean that you must remain resolute, and hold out for what you know to be right for you. You must resist intimidation.

radio A dream of listening to the radio can mean that you should try to increase your receptivity to difficult, shocking or dangerous ideas.

rain Rain can symbolize a happy social time with good friends, good conversation and plenty of food and drink. If you are soon to host a party, be assured that it will go well.

rainbow Despite their great beauty, rainbows in dreams can be signs of bad luck, especially if your dream featured pointing at a rainbow. You need to be especially careful when doing calculations of any sort, as rainbows can symbolize mistakes in arithmetic.

razor What kind of razor (or electric shaver) was it? Blunt or sharp? Clean or dirty? Were you shaving, or watching someone being shaved? Factors such as these must be taken into account, but often a razor, of any type, signifies your ability to cut through a tangled mass of confusion to reach a clearer perspective on an intellectual problem. Any sort of dirty or rusty razor can be a warning against the dangers of sloppy personal hygiene.

reading What was being read? A book, newspaper, or magazine? Who was reading and were they reading silently or aloud? Think about questions such as this before you attempt an interpretation. In general, reading symbolizes steady progress on, and a growing insight into, a problem that is bothering you.

referee *See* umpire.

relatives The meaning of your dream will depend largely on your relationship with your actual relatives. If these are cordial, such a dream may signify that your relatives will be a source of help in times of need; if they are not cordial, the dream may be prompting you to attempt to patch up a family feud before it is too late. *See also* individual entries for family members.

repetition If your dream features many repetitions, whatever is its underlying meaning is doubly emphasized – your subconscious is not satisfied with telling you something once, but feels it must repeat the message.

rescue By the mechanism of contraries, dreams of rescue often concern abandonment, literal or metaphorical. Have you ever been literally abandoned, for example by a parent or lover? If so, this dream could be working on themes relating to this incident – loss, grief, a sense of betrayal, etc. Have you ever abandoned anybody? If so, this dream is asking you to confront your actions and make appropriate amends, if possible, especially if children are involved.

resigning A dream of resignation often heralds a promotion at work, or public recognition of an achievement you thought had been overlooked.

rice Rice can symbolize domestic happiness, children and health. It is a lucky symbol.

ring A ring can symbolize cure for minor ailments, especially if it is given to you by a member of the opposite sex. The giving and receiving of rings by men and women can, in dreams, symbolize the need for harmony between the masculine and feminine aspects of your personality. *See also* engaged couple/engagement ring *and* wedding/cake/ring.

river According to the Hippocratic treatise *On Regimen*, a river stands for the dreamer's blood. A river can also stand for flux in one's life, as it is never the same from moment to moment. A river carries things into and out of one's life – good things and bad things alike. It can thus symbolize good things to come or the loss of good things, trouble to come or troubles washed away. *See* Louise's dreams, Chapter 3.

road Roads can symbolize literal journeys in a quite straightforward way, as well as spiritual or emotional growth. Roadblocks, or busy city roads filled with traffic, can symbolize obstacles on the journey. Quiet country roads can symbolize peace on the journey or at its destination. A fork in the road suggests that you are about to be faced with a significant choice. A crossroads can indicate multiple opportunities. A dead end can indicate that you are on the wrong track when it comes to solving a problem. If you are tempted to turn off the main road on to a side road, beware being side-tracked while trying to achieve your journey's destination.

rolling pin To dream of a rolling pin, especially of using one, is a good sign, especially if you are about to undertake travel. It can suggest a safe journey.

room The meaning depends on the type of room and the type of building. But, in general, upper rooms are unlucky signs in a dream. For more on rooms, *see* India's diary, Chapter 2.

rope Dreams of rope, especially, by the mechanism of contraries, rope nooses, can symbolize evil averted. Alternatively, rope can symbolize frustration and the sense that you have few choices or alternatives in life, and have sacrificed too much of your freedom. If you dream of rope while engaged in sensitive negotiations, they will end in an agreement that is favourable to you.

rubbish/refuse You are probably being warned against hoarding and overconsumption. Think about sorting through your possessions and giving any unwanted clothes, books, CDs or other items to charity.

ruins To dream of ruins can symbolize dilapidation in your own life. This could be physical – you need to pay attention to your diet and exercise regime – emotional or spiritual. In any event, you need to take firm action to prevent further deterioration.

running Who is doing the running, and why? The meaning will vary according to other details in the dream, but often dreams of running symbolize the need to organize and prioritize your use of time. You need to draw up some firm agendas and action plans if you are not to be overwhelmed by all the various tasks you have to perform.

rust If you dream of rusty implements, expect to receive a gift of money.

S

sailors To dream of a sailor foretells good luck.

salt To dream of salt could suggest that you will soon be asked to make amends for a wrong you have done. Alternatively, it can be a sign of a financial gain, or of protection against as yet unrecognized forces of ill will, including ill will towards children and animals. If you dream of being offered salt, and accepting it, you can expect sorrow to come into your life. If you dream of offering salt to another, the two of you are likely to quarrel. To dream of spilling salt can suggest anger. To dream of breaking a salt cellar is an unlucky sign.

Senses and sensations

A dream that features any of your senses performing well – you can see, hear, taste, smell or feel things more intensely than usual – usually symbolizes intuition or feeling – our non-rational natures. Dreams of heightened sensation, or of odd sensations, or of mistakes in perception, can all indicate that you are about to enter a period of heightened awareness of things spiritual or metaphysical, and that you will be able to detect meanings and patterns where you saw none before. New insights of a general nature could be revealed to you, or you may receive insight into a specific problem that has been bothering you. Such dreams can also concern your sensibility – your capacity to feel. They could indicate exceptional openness to emotional impressions, so watch out that your feelings don't get hurt and don't be too quick to take offence. Dreams featuring senses are sometimes linked to your sensuality and can indicate that you will soon be enjoying all the pleasures of carnal self-indulgence, or they could carry a warning that you should not get too wedded to the pursuit of fleshly gratification.

scissors If you dream of giving or receiving scissors as a gift, expect the end of a friendship or a relationship. To dream of dropping scissors can foretell a house move, or the coming of a stranger. If the scissors fall and the point sticks in the ground, you can expect an increase in your workload.

sea *See* ocean.

seasonable/unseasonable In general, to dream of anything outside its natural season means trouble of one sort or another.

seaweed Seaweed can be a warning against fire – check your smoke alarms, or install some if you do not already have them.

seeds Seeds can be a fairly obvious symbol for new beginnings and new enterprises, or of a new idea that will be important in your life, for good or ill.

selling To dream of selling something can be a sign that your health will soon take a turn for the worse, but only for a short time.

sex *See* Chapter 6.

shadows The meaning depends almost entirely on the context of your dream, but shadows can often herald ill health or other bad luck.

shark A traditional symbol of terror, generally an omen of danger – *see* Edward's dream, Chapter 4. *See also* Animals *and* Fish.

shoelace A broken shoelace can be a symbol of a safe journey with a successful outcome. To dream of a shoelace becoming untied, but not breaking, can herald bad luck, as can a dream of giving or receiving a shoelace.

shoes It is important to note whether the shoes were old or new. To dream of buying new shoes can foretell a loss of a treasured possession, or the loss of a friendship. Dreams of new shoes can also be an omen of very bad weather, so bear this in mind if you are planning a long journey. If you dream of walking in new shoes that squeak, you can expect to be asked to repay an old debt. Old shoes have far more positive meanings. Old shoes can represent good luck, especially in a new romance or in a new house. They can also represent healing and the power to avert minor inconveniences.

shopping This can be a straightforward symbol of waste and extravagance, telling you to be more careful about what you choose to consume. Or it may be concerned with the need to pay more attention to your budget and be more careful with your financial resources. Shopping dreams often have to do with wish fulfilment. *See* Louise's dream, Chapter 3.

shroud By the mechanism of contraries, this is not a dream symbol to be dreaded. You will need to determine the exact meaning according to the context and your circumstances, but expect happiness.

singing Who was singing, and why and when? Was it operatic singing, hymn singing, folksongs, or what? You need to be aware of questions such as these when trying to determine the meaning. But, in general, if you dream of singing yourself, you can expect some good news. If you dreamed of hearing someone else singing in an informal context, expect to hear that a friend or loved one has received good news. But the timing is important: if, in your dream, the singing occurs early in the morning, the meaning is that disappointing news is coming. For operatic singing, *see* opera.

sister A dream of your sister can be a symbol of rivalry – not necessarily with your sister but, perhaps, at work or in a sporting context. It could also indicate the necessity of asking for, or offering, emotional support. *See also* brother.

skiing Dreams of skiing often concern the need for balance in some aspect of your life. *See* Mary's dream, Chapter 5.

skull By the mechanism of contraries, this is not a grim dream and is often concerned with healing. However, to dream of picking up a skull and moving it from one place to another can herald bad luck.

sleeping To dream of sleeping alone can indicate a period of rejuvenation in your life. The meaning of a dream about sleeping with another depends on who that other person was, and his or her relationship to you.

sneezing The number of times you sneeze in a dream, or witness another sneeze, has often been thought to have divinatory significance. For example, two sneezes have been thought to suggest good luck in business. Keep a careful record in your dream diary, and see if the number of sneezes has any significance for you.

soap Something in your life will be hard to get, attain or achieve, but perseverance will pay off.

son *See* child/children *and* Mary's dream, Chapter 5.

spade You need to face up to reality and tell the truth about some matter. If you are carrying a spade inside a building, that can indicate coming trouble. Digging with a spade can indicate frustration.

spices To dream of spices can indicate a great age difference between two partners in a relationship.

spitting It is generally lucky to witness someone spitting in a dream, and can indicate a financial gain, good health and protection from harm. However, if you were the one doing the spitting, beware of offending others through thoughtless behaviour.

spoons If you are single, a dream of spoons can herald a new relationship. If you are in a relationship that appears to be faltering, the appearance of spoons in your dream is an assurance that soon all will be well.

staff/rod A symbol of wisdom and wise counsel. Do not dismiss advice given to you in the following few days, even if at first you are reluctant to listen.

staircase It can be an unlucky sign if you dream of meeting someone on stairs, or of turning round to go down, once you have started up the stairs. *See also* stumbling. The discussion of Freud in Chapter 7 gives the possible sexual connotations of this dream symbol.

star Shooting stars are significant symbols, although they mean different things for different people. Diametrically opposed interpretations, such as a birth or a death, a celebration or a disaster, are not impossible. Stars can symbolize wishes granted. It is an unlucky portent if you dream of pointing at the stars, or trying to count them. Trying to count the stars is a sign of arrogance.

stealing Were you the thief or the victim? If the thief, was your wrongdoing discovered? These are all relevant considerations when trying to determine the meaning of a dream about stealing. In general, if you were the thief, beware a destructive jealousy that could make you unhappy over the coming months. If you were the victim, are you guilty of hoarding something that ought to be shared (e.g. information)?

stones In dreams, stones can sometimes symbolize the self, especially the higher self, the mind or soul.

storm A storm can be a straightforward symbol of forces that you cannot control, and which will buffet your life over the coming weeks. It can be a warning to plan ahead and try to build yourself a storm-proof shelter, in which to hide until life calms down once more.

stranger By the mechanism of contraries, dreams of strangers often concern close and intimate friends. You will have to determine the exact details from the context of your dream. *See also* Louise's dream, Chapter 3.

strength By the mechanism of contraries, dreams of strength can symbolize weakness.

string This can be a lucky dream, concerning friends and money.

stumbling Stumbling in a dream can be a symbol of guilt. Are you hiding some unconfessed wrong? To dream-stumble as you are going upstairs can indicate a wedding – yours or someone else's; to stumble coming down can be a sign of ill luck. To dream-stumble in a graveyard can be an unlucky portent. To dream of stumbling in a theatre, cinema or concert hall can foretell the success of a new enterprise.

sugar Try to be less cloying in your relations with others, as your apparent sweetness is enough to give those you deal with toothache! Spilt sugar in a dream can be a sign of good luck.

sun The sun can be a powerful symbol, standing for rationality and the light of consciousness, as well as light and energy considered in a literal sense. To dream of the rising or the setting of the sun can symbolize new beginnings and new opportunities. It is unlucky to dream of pointing at the sun.

The sun can also symbolize danger from fire, or danger from fire narrowly averted.

sword It is unlucky to dream of a sword falling from its scabbard. Otherwise, dreams of swords are often concerned with the need to separate truth from falsehood, right from wrong, justice from injustice, and other polarities.

T

table/tablecloth/table napkin If you are single and dream of sitting on a table, that can be a sign that you are ready for a new relationship. If you are in a relationship, it can be a sign that the relationship is in trouble. If you dream of two people sitting at a table, that can mean a quarrel. Depending on the context of the dream, a tablecloth can signal ill health. To dream of folding a table napkin can suggest you are about to leave a place, or a job, for good.

tea/tea pot/tea leaves If you dream of making tea, the strength of the brew can be significant. Weak tea can symbolize a broken friendship; strong tea a new friendship. Spilling tea can herald good luck, but stirring it can herald ill fortune. If you dream of tea with many leaves floating on the top, or of a teapot, that can suggest that a stranger is about to come into your life.

teeth Commonly, anxiety expresses itself in dreams of all the dreamer's teeth dropping out. If you dream of your teeth dropping out, this can herald bad luck for someone close to you. To dream of someone with gaps between their teeth can be a sign of prosperity. *See also* dentist.

telephone Sometimes the rings of an actual telephone can cause you to dream of a telephone ringing. If this is not the case, this can be a sign of ill fortune, especially ill health.

theatre If you work in the theatre, this may be a neutral symbol reflecting your everyday activities. For others, to dream of appearing in a play, or a film, can be a sign that a new venture will fail. Dreams about applying theatrical make-up also suggest bad luck. To dream of an empty stage can herald a new contract of some sort. Dreams of theatre tickets can symbolize frustration. *See also* opera *and* stumbling.

thieves *See* stealing.

Toys

If you are a parent, a dream of toys can merely reflect the contents of your house. Contrariwise, toys can sometimes suggest that you are acting immaturely with respect to a difficult problem, or failing to treat a situation with the seriousness it deserves. Dreams of toys can sometimes indicate that you are making too much of some trifling inconvenience. Specific toys often carry warnings – don't forget, it all depends on context, and on the circumstances of your life, but here are some pointers. **Teddy bears:** beware of people misinterpreting themselves to you. **Dolls:** beware of shabby or fake goods being passed off as the real thing. **Dolls' houses:** beware of leading someone on, especially a member of the opposite sex. **Toy soldiers:** beware of picking fights, when there is no real fighting to be done. **Soft toys:** beware of playing with ideas – you must come to a decision and act firmly, if you feel like picking an argument. **Puzzles:** beware of being wasteful.

thorns To dream of thorns can be a powerful symbol of healing and protection, or of happiness in a relationship. Sometimes, depending on the context, thorns can symbolize obstacles or difficulties, or the need to disentangle yourself from a difficult situation.

thread If you dream of removing a thread from someone's clothes, expect to receive a present or a letter. If you are about to travel and dream of winding thread, this can foretell a difficult and frustrating journey.

tidal waves/tornadoes By the mechanism of contraries, a tidal wave or a tornado, both of which are destructive, can symbolize opportunities, new enterprises and new beginnings.

tigers *See* Animals and Louise's dream, Chapter 3.

tongs Sugar tongs, barbeque tongs, coal tongs, etc., all carry a warning against trying to interfere in other people's business – don't be a nosey parker, and don't try to be bossy, or run other people's lives. Tongs also indicate secrets, especially secret meetings.

tools Tools of any sort can symbolize your practical nature and the necessity for self-reliance. However, the exact interpretation will depend on the type of tool, your personal circumstances and the dream context.

traffic Often a sign of obstacles on your path to success, or of wasted resources – emotional and spiritual as well as physical. *See* Edward's dream, Chapter 4.

trains It is often claimed that trains and tunnels have a sexual connotation, but you do not have to accept such an interpretation; *see* Louise's dream, Chapter 5.

travel *See* journey.

tree According to the Hippocratic treatise *On Regimen*, a tree stands for the dreamer's reproductive system. It can also stand for channels of communication. If you dream of a tree, do you need to improve your communication skills?

twins If you are a twin, or a parent of twins, the significance of this dream depends almost entirely on your relationship with your twin, or with your children. For others, twins can symbolize rivalry, especially between the generations (e.g. between father and son).

U

. . . .

ugliness To dream of a person repulsive to sight can indicate that you are about to come up against a formidable, and intellectually very able, opponent, who will pose a distinct threat to your plans.

umbrella An umbrella is often a symbol of a quarrel, or of the failure of an enterprise. If you dream of dropping an umbrella, you can expect a decision to be given against you.

umpire A dream of a cricket umpire, or of any kind of referee, all indicate conflict and its resolution. They can indicate that you will soon be asked to give judgement on some issue, or to enforce the rules, or to decide disputes.

uncle The meaning depends, to a large extent, on your relationship with your uncles and on the surrounding symbols. Freedom from worry may be indicated.

undertaker By the mechanism of contraries, this often symbolizes a celebration or a new beginning. It can also be a prompt that you should repay old debts.

undressing Who was undressing? What were the circumstances? Were the people undressing of the same sex as you? Did the scene take place in public? These are the sorts of questions you must ask before attempting an interpretation. In general, to dream of oneself undressing can indicate that you should try to be more trusting of someone in your life. Dreams of seeing someone else undressing often concern balance and gender. To see someone of the same sex as you undressing is a prompt that you should rein in the masculine side of your nature if you are a man, or the feminine side if you are a woman. To dream of seeing someone of the opposite sex undressing suggests you should be more aware of how the feminine plays out in your life if you are a man, or how the masculine manifests in you if you are a woman.

unicorn A symbol of virtue and positive spiritual values, or positive human attributes or emotions, the unicorn frequently has religious connotations. Think especially about the role of forgiveness and redemption in your life. *See* the discussion in Chapter 4.

uniform If you habitually wear a uniform, such a dream will have a different meaning for you than for others and may be insignificant. If you do not usually wear a uniform, it is important to note the type of uniform and the circumstances. Often, uniforms represent the power of social constraint, but whether your dream is telling you to pay more or less heed to this force depends on your circumstances and the dream context.

university This can symbolize your own power to think through a problem and come up with a solution, or warn you that someone is trying to bamboozle you with sophisticated, but misleading, arguments.

unmarried man Are you male or female, single or not? If you are a single man, take this as a warning to be careful about how you choose your friends, male and female. If you are in a relationship, take it as a warning that you need to make more effort if you want to keep your partner happy. If you are a single woman, this could be a sign that you are about to enter a new relationship. If you are a woman in a relationship, take it as a warning against infidelity.

unmarried woman Are you male or female, single or not? If you are a single woman, take this as a warning to be careful about how you choose your friends, male and female. If you are in a relationship, take it as a warning that you need to make more effort if you want to keep your partner happy. If you are a single man, this could be a sign that you are about to enter a new relationship. If you are a man in a relationship, take it as a warning against infidelity.

urine/urination These can be symbols of protection and financial security.

V

Vegetables

Depending on surrounding symbols, the humble still-growing or recently harvested vegetable can often stand for spiritual regeneration and rejuvenation. The dream could be telling you to pay more attention to your spiritual growth. Buying or selling vegetables can be a warning against squandering your spiritual reserves. Cooking or eating vegetables can be concerned with your role in nurturing others engaged in their own spiritual quests. Vegetables often symbolize love or friendship. Individual vegetables can have the following meanings, mostly connected with not taking the good things we have for granted. But remember, all meanings are subjective. **Carrots/parsnips:** treasure your happy home life. **Turnips:** be grateful for the help of strangers. **Onions/garlic:** treasure your good health. **Cabbage:** treasure your partner. **Broccoli:** treasure your children. **Potatoes:** treasure small kindnesses. **Leeks:** treasure your friends. **Pumpkin:** treasure yourself.

vaccination Did you administer the jab, receive it, or merely witness it? If you administered a jab, and you are not, in waking life, qualified to do so, take it as a warning against trying to impress others by exaggerating your skills, position, CV, etc. If you received a jab, you are being warned to take simple precautions to protect your wellbeing – emotional, spiritual and mental. If you merely witnessed someone being vaccinated, take this as a hint that you should be more charitable in your dealings with others. The meaning of this symbol will change if you are strongly opposed to vaccination, or if you are a doctor or a nurse.

Valentine's Day If you dream of Valentine's Day at any other time of the year, this probably heralds a period of emotional turmoil. If you dream of Valentine's Day around about 14 February, take this as a positive sign for a new or existing relationship. By the mechanism of contraries, if you dream of receiving many cards, you will not get many, but if you dream of being left out, somebody admires you from afar even though he or she may be shy about admitting this. If you dream about sending a Valentine's card, you are being prompted into taking positive action to force the pace in a sluggish relationship.

vampire This dream may be warning you against some undertaking that would be expedient, but which you know to be against your own interests and opposed to your deepest values. It is telling you to recognize the value of integrity.

veil This can mean that you will soon have the solution to a problem that has been tormenting you, or that you will soon see how to make a significant choice, and why.

village For city dwellers, this can be a straightforward symbol of the power of nostalgia and a warning not to become too obsessed by the past. For people who actually live in villages, it can be a warning against becoming overly parochial in their attitudes and concerns.

vine/vineyard In either case, you could be being warned against excessive, or risky, gambling.

violence Were you the perpetrator, the victim, or merely a witness? If you were the perpetrator, carefully think about your reaction to the violence, both in your dream and in your waking life. Remember that some activities are exciting only if they remain in the realm of dreams, where social constraints do not apply. If you think you are in any danger of acting out violent dreams, consult your family doctor. If you were the victim of violence, you need to try to become more aware of your own worth; perhaps you would benefit from some assertiveness training. If you witnessed violence and did nothing, you are being warned against indifference in the face of others' suffering. If you intervened, you are being warned not to be reckless with your own safety – physical, emotional or spiritual.

virgin The meaning will change depending on your sex and on whether or not you are a virgin. In general, however, virgins of either sex are powerful symbols of healing and protection.

visitor Were you the visitor or the host? To dream of receiving a visitor can herald good news; to dream of visiting someone can mean that you will soon be carrying welcome news to another.

volcano As a symbol, an erupting volcano is commonly thought to have sexual connotations. It can also symbolize any aspect of your personality that you have repressed to such an extent that an eruption is likely. An inactive volcano can be telling you that you need to slow down and accept a period of stasis in your life.

volunteer If you dream of volunteering for a job, that is generally an unlucky sign.

vomiting This can be a warning against repeating past mistakes, or an indication that you are about to be made to pay for a past indiscretion.

voting A straightforward symbol of your role as a citizen. Are you neglecting your political duties, or failing to take any interest? If so, the dream is telling you to get involved, and start paying attention to the problems of your community.

vow To dream of taking a vow can mean that you will soon break one.

W
. . . .

walking If you dream of walking forwards confidently, you can expect to triumph over another in a competitive context. If you dream of walking backwards, that suggests failure in a competitive context.

warts Warts can symbolize that you worry too much about your looks. Others find you beautiful.

washing If you are about to embark on a journey, washing clothes can symbolize the wisdom of delaying your trip, for some reason. To dream of making a terrible mess while washing clothes could be a sign that someone close to you has a problem with alcohol. If you dream of washing your hands at the same sink as another, that can symbolize a quarrel. To dream of washing pots and pans together can symbolize harmony between two people.

water You need to pay careful attention to the surrounding detail before attempting an interpretation but, in general, water is a symbol of purification. Deep water symbolizes the need to try to drag something to consciousness from the depths of your subconscious. Shallow water warns against making snap judgements. Muddy water can symbolize clouded or destructive emotions or clouded judgement. Running water can indicate that you need to become more fluid in your thinking. Stagnant water can indicate the need to make radical changes in your life.

wax Dreams of wax – wax candles, wax polishes, beeswax – can all indicate that you need to ask difficult questions and be brave enough to follow through on the answers. Wax can also symbolize anger, or that you are about to pass into a new mood, which will dominate your life for a while.

weakness By the mechanism of contraries, dreams of weakness often symbolize strength.

wedding/cake/ring The meaning of dreams concerned with weddings depends largely on your own personal circumstances and on surrounding symbols. However, to dream of a wedding often foretells an actual wedding; to dream of a wedding cake often foretells a birth. If you are married, it is exceedingly unlucky to dream of taking off your wedding ring.

weeping By the mechanism of contraries, this often means you will soon be experiencing joy.

weighing *See* measuring.

well To dream of a well suggests good health and financial prosperity.

widow/widower To dream of a widow or a widower often means you are searching for balance between intuition and rationality in your thinking. Remember that both are needed if you are to make sensible decisions.

wig A wig can be a warning against falsity.

wind A warm and gentle breeze can foretell good news. A brisk breeze can symbolize new attitudes, ideas or feelings. A wind that blows strongly, dies down, then picks up again indicates that you will reach a goal only after several periods of frustration. A gale indicates extreme difficulty in reaching your goals. *See also* Louise's dream, Chapter 5.

wine This can symbolize the power of friendship, especially friendships with people of the same sex as you. If a drinking party becomes rowdy, you are being warned against being led astray by bad company.

witches/wizards and warlocks The meaning will depend on your personal circumstances, especially your gender, and surrounding details in your dream, but, in general, these characters are a warning not to take things at face value, or to make snap judgements, but to adopt a questioning, critical stance in trying to arrive at the truth concerning any matter.

woman The meaning depends on the context. Sometimes women warn against treachery and deceit; sometimes they symbolize huge gains in your life. *See also* man.

wound To dream of being wounded can be a straightforward sign that others wish you ill. To dream of inflicting a wound can be a symbol of your simmering frustration with an aspect of your life – try to make changes before it is too late.

X / Y / Z

x-rays If you dream of looking at x-rays, expect sudden insight into a very challenging intellectual problem. If you dream of being x-rayed, this could be a simple expression of anxiety, but take the hint seriously if you have any worrying symptoms and consult your family doctor.

xylophone A dream of a xylophone can symbolize forest, woods and trees. In very general terms, a xylophone can be interpreted as a call to protect the environment or think about environmental issues.

yacht If you dream of observing, owning or sailing on a luxurious yacht, then by the mechanism of contraries expect a period of financial hardship. If you dream of a more simple sailing craft, expect financial gain to follow on the heels of hard work.

yard *See* garden/gardening.

yarn To dream of winding yarn, or wool, suggests a new friendship. *See also* thread.

yawning To dream of yawning can be a sign that you are at risk from menacing forces, which you will find it difficult to identify. Be on your guard.

yeti Dreams of long-haired, grunting yetis can indicate that we should pay more attention to the wisdom contained in traditional cultures, and not assume that our technological advanced society has all the answers.

Zodiac

The full meaning will depend on the details of your birth chart – if you know only your sun sign, your interpretation will inevitably be shallow. But, in general, to dream of seeing all the signs of the zodiac suggests success in some enterprise. A creative or artistic project could bring unexpected financial reward. The signs of the zodiac mean different things to different people, but here are some hints. **Aries:** you need to be more questioning about life. **Taurus:** do not rely on brute strength to get you through a crisis. **Gemini:** try to be consistent in the presentation of your views. **Cancer:** don't pretend you are emotionally tougher than you really are. **Leo:** guard against arrogance. **Virgo:** do not set your beloved up on a pedestal. **Libra:** watch out for deception. **Scorpio:** pay more attention to your sensual needs. **Sagittarius:** don't set yourself unattainable goals; be realistic. **Capricorn:** guard against stubbornness.

Aquarius: be more open to the mystical. **Pisces:** do not let the good things in your life slip through your fingers through carelessness. Depending on circumstance, any of the zodiac signs can symbolize animals – perhaps such a dream could really be about one of your domestic pets.

yoga If you habitually practise yoga, this could be a neutral symbol. For others, to dream either of doing yoga exercises yourself, or of watching someone else, both hint that you are overstressed, overcommitted and suffering from poor time management. You need to make time for yourself, for your family and for relaxation.

youth Dreams of your youth are almost always significant, but the meaning will depend entirely on your personal circumstances and the details of the dream. If you dream of a youth known to you, the details of your relationship determine the meaning. An unknown youth can be an archetypal symbol of strength, forgiveness and trust – qualities you may need to develop in your daily life. A youth can also symbolize a spiritual quest.

zeal/zealot Sometimes excessive zeal in a dream situation is a hint that we are becoming too fanatical or prejudiced in our thinking.

zebra A symbol of nervousness, even paranoia. Try to calm down. Beware of deception.

zebra crossing This can mean that you are neglecting your duties to others. Consider whether this might apply to you.

zip This can be a dream hinting at minor difficulties in reaching a goal, or at the need for discretion in your personal affairs.

zoo A zoo can symbolize the need to husband your resources efficiently, and to care for your immediate environment. To dream of taking children to the zoo is a lucky portent, foretelling happiness in the domestic sphere.

Taking it further

Further reading

Berry, R., *Freud: A Beginner's Guide*, Headway, 2000. Useful introduction.

Berry, R., *Jung: A Beginner's Guide*, Headway, 2000. Useful introduction.

Browne, S., *Sylvia Browne's Book of Dreams*, Dutton, 2002. Good all-round introduction.

Dodds, E.R., *The Greeks and the Irrational*, University of California Press, 1951. Fascinating account of Greek thinking about the irrational.

Freud, S., *The Interpretation of Dreams* (various editions). A must-read classic.

Goldberg, B., *Dream Your Problems Away*, New Page Books, 2003. Heal yourself while you sleep.

Holloway, G., *Dreaming Insights*, Psychology Press, 2002. A five-step plan for discovering the meaning in your dreams.

Jung, C.G., *The Archetypes and the Collective Unconscious* (various editions).

Jung, C.G., *Man and His Symbols* (various editions)

Jung, C.G., *Memories, Dreams, Reflections* (various editions)

All three Jung books are must-read classics.

Koch-Sheras, P.R. and Sheras, P.L., *The Dream Sharing Sourcebook*, Lowell House, 1998. Husband-and-wife team share insights.

Krippner, S. and Waldman, M.R., *Dreamscaping*, Lowell House, 1999. New techniques for understanding yourself and others.

McPhee, C.L., *Ask the Dream Doctor: An A–Z guide to deciphering the hidden symbols of your dreams*, Delta, 2002

Opie, I. and Tatem, M., *A Dictionary of Superstitions*, Oxford University Press, 1992. Another slant on symbols, including details of superstitions linked to dreams.

Stevens, A., *Jung: A Very Short Introduction*, Oxford University Press, 2001. Useful introduction.

Storr, A., *Freud: A Very Short Introduction*, Oxford University Press, 2001. Useful introduction.

Sun Bear, *Dreaming with the Wheel: How to interpret and work with your dreams using the medicine wheel*, Simon & Schuster, 1994

Websites

Hundreds of websites are devoted to dream interpretation, very many of which have been established by dreamers who are willing to share their dreams. The live sites change very quickly, and new ones are set up all the time. For these reasons I am not making specific suggestions about websites you should visit. However, the Internet is a very rich resource for dreamers and can provide an online community offering support and a chance to explore different ideas, especially about the interpretation of specific symbols. The best way of tapping into this resource is to get surfing! If you do not have access to the Internet at home, try your local library.